SPEED BREWING

TECHNIQUES AND RECIPES
FOR FAST-FERMENTING BEERS,
CIDERS, MEADS, AND MORE

MARY IZETT

Voyageur
Press

CONTENTS

INTRODUCTION

I USED TO BE a traditional homebrewer. I brewed a lot of beer and made the occasional cider and I loved every part of the process—from planning my recipe to smelling the sweet aroma of grain being mashed to hearing the sound of the airlock bubbling away as my beer fermented. And who doesn't love drinking and sharing the finished beers? Yet if beer brewing has one downside, it's this: it takes a good amount of time. Like most other brewers I know, I had to dedicate a precious weekend day to brew and then more time to monitor the fermentation and bottle the beers.

As weeks turned into months, and months turned into years, my life continued to change and I didn't always have a full day off to brew, so I started looking for ways to brew the same high-quality beer in fewer hours. Around the same time that I started seeking maximum brewing efficiency, I also started exploring a variety of other alcoholic beverages that not only took significantly less time to make, but also finished their fermentation faster.

My first success off the beaten path came with short meads. They were fast, easy, and (most importantly) delightfully tasty! I could brew them whenever I didn't have time to brew beer, when all of my carboys were full, or when I just craved a little

something different. They were also fun to bring to festivals and other beer-centric events, since they stood out from the other beverages.

Soon I was receiving more requests for my short mead recipes than for my beer! Nonbrewers wanted to know if they could make one, and even die-hard beer brewers were interested in making a batch of their own. As you'll see in this book, short meads were just the beginning. I went all the way down the rabbit hole and learned how to make unique ciders as well as boozy versions of sodas, kombucha, water kefir, and more. While the flavors vary wildly, and while each lets you play with ingredients and process in a different way, these

beverages have one thing in common—they all take a minimal time investment on brew day.

The other part of my speed brewing philosophy is optional, but I highly recommend trying it before you dismiss it: brew small batches, from a half gallon to two and a half gallons depending on the beverage. Brewing at half the conventional batch size (or less) cuts down on time for the rest of the brewing process. Fermentations tend to finish faster, or at the very least your beverages will taste great and be ready to drink sooner. Smaller batch sizes also allow you to have a greater variety of beverages on hand with the same amount of equipment and space. And if something doesn't turn out exactly as you pictured it, you're not too crushed if you've only made a gallon!

I find that experienced homebrewers are often skeptical about these easy, fast fermentations. I was, too, at first! If you had told me ten years ago I could add champagne yeast to sweet jasmine tea, ferment it for a mere seven days, bottle it, and then drink a freaking fantastic beverage two days later, I would have laughed. It just doesn't seem right! But let me assure you, it works. If it helps you get over the mental hump, remember that humans have been making fast-fermented beverages with whatever we've had on hand and drinking them fresh for thousands of years.

If nothing else, keep an open mind as you explore this book. Make a gallon here and a gallon there and find out what flavors work for you (and for your family and friends, of course). You may find you dislike meads of all kinds but love herbal sodas with a kick. Or as a sour beer drinker, you may quickly become obsessed with SCOBY fermentations. Whatever the case may be, I hope that this book helps you keep brewing no matter how busy life gets.

—Mary Izett

1

GETTING STARTED

I N BROAD TERMS, this book is all about fermentation. To be technical about it, fermentation is the process of converting sugars to alcohol, gases, and organic acids. Organisms such as yeast actually ferment in order to produce energy for themselves—alcohols, gases, and acids are merely byproducts of the fermentation process. But what splendid byproducts they are!

On the pages that follow, we'll cover the basic brewing ingredients and equipment you'll need for most of the fermentations in this book. We'll also cover the basics of bottling. However, because each chapter deals with a different class of beverages, each chapter has its own unique brewing process. That means you'll find your basic beer brew day in Chapter 2, page 33, whereas your brew day for boozy buch is in Chapter 5, page 115.

Between this basics chapter and the beverage chapters that follow, you will be able to brew and bottle anything in this book. However, if you get bitten by the brewing bug, I highly recommend you read a more comprehensive brewing book or two, such as *How to Brew* by John Palmer, *The Complete Joy of Homebrewing* by Charlie Papazian, *The Compleat Meadmaker* by Ken Schramm, and *The Everything Hard Cider Book* by Drew Beechum.

INGREDIENTS

Yeast

In this book, we will be taking advantage of the magical power of yeast (okay, mostly yeast) to ferment sugar into carbon dioxide and alcohol. So let's look a little closer into that process.

Yeast are relatively simple organisms in the biologic world—single-celled fungi that reproduce asexually by either mitosis or budding. We primarily will be using a species of yeast named *Saccharomyces cerevisiae*. *S. cerevisiae* are found in nature on the skins of grapes and other fruit and are used to make alcoholic beverages such as beer, wine, cider, and mead and are also the most common species used in bread making. They can consume a variety of sugars—including glucose, sucrose, maltose, and fructose—to produce not only carbon dioxide and ethanol but also a wide variety of other compounds that contribute to the aroma and flavor of the finished beverage. These yeast need certain environmental conditions and nutrients in order to exist and thrive. Controlling and manipulating the food source (type, or types, of sugar) as well as the environment affects the resulting level of alcohol and carbon dioxide, the aroma, and the flavor of your finished beverage. One might compare creating an alcoholic beverage to building a house for your yeast from start to finish: you're the architect, contractor, builder, electrician, plumber, and interior designer all in one. In brewing terms, you're designing the recipe; building a desirable substrate, or food for your yeast; and providing the proper environment through controlling the temperature, oxygen, light, and nutrients.

There are many different yeast strains under the *S. cerevisiae* species umbrella, and they can all affect your beverage in different ways, including alcohol strength, clarity, aroma, and flavor. The majority of the recipes in this book call for an American ale, English ale, or champagne yeast, which are easy to work with and are comfortable in a wide range of environmental conditions. Besides sugar, they require some basic nutrients in order to do their job. Your raw ingredients might contain all of the nutrients required to keep your yeast happy, or you might need to add some. Ale yeast prefer room-temperature conditions, generally between 59°F and 75°F, while champagne yeast is more tolerant, working well between 45°F and 95°F. Yeast require oxygen, but this is

9

smaller batches, has a longer shelf life, is less expensive, and contains more yeast cells in each packet. However, wet yeast comes in many more varieties and may be used in almost all of the recipes in this book, especially those in the beer chapter. Whereas wet yeast comes ready to pitch—that is, ready to add to your fermenter—dry yeast benefits from rehydration and even more so from rehydration with a rehydration nutrient. When brewing small, low-alcohol fast fermentations, I often pitch dry yeast directly into the wort or substrate. However, pitching dry yeast directly into the sugar substrate may reduce its viability, so I add extra yeast (a tactic known as overpitching) to compensate. I always rehydrate with yeast rehydration nutrient when making acidic beverages, such as sima and boozy buch. The bottom line is that rehydrating dry yeast with a rehydration nutrient is optimal, rehydrating with water is recommended, and overpitching directly onto your substrate is acceptable for low-alcohol fast fermentations.

To rehydrate dry yeast with water only, you'll need an amount of water ten times the weight of the yeast you're pitching. It's best to use preboiled tap water instead of filtered or distilled water when rehydrating yeast—you need at least some mineral

easily provided for the small-batch, low-alcohol ferments in this book by agitating or shaking the substrate. Champagne yeast is also quite tolerant of acidic or low-pH environments, which we will be creating for a few of the recipes.

Yeast for homebrewers comes in dry and wet forms, and both types have their pros and cons. I use a lot of dry yeast because it's easier to measure out for content in the water you use for rehydration or you'll run into problems, and distilled and filtered water have almost none.

1. Allow your yeast packet to come to room temperature.
2. Heat water in a microwave or on a burner to between 95°F and 104°F.
3. Place a sterile, heat-resistant, microwaveable container on the scale and zero it out.
4. Add water to the container until the scale reads ten times the weight of the yeast you will be using.
5. Sprinkle the yeast evenly on top, avoiding clumps.
6. Cover with plastic wrap and wait 15 minutes.
7. Uncover, gently stir with a sanitized spoon, and recover.
8. Yeast is ready to pitch once the temperature drops to the desired yeast pitching/fermentation temperature. It should not rehydrate for more than 30 minutes.

To rehydrate dry yeast with yeast rehydration nutrient, you'll use 1.25 grams of the nutrient (these instructions are based on using Go-Ferm) per 1 gram of yeast and rehydrate in water that is twenty times the weight of the Go-Ferm and ten times the weight of the yeast you're pitching. It is still best to use preboiled tap water instead of filtered or distilled water when rehydrating.

REHYDRATING YEAST WITH WATER

Weight of yeast	Weight of water required	Approximate volume of water
1.25g (¼ of a 5g packet)	12.5g	2½ tsp.
1.67g (¼ of an 11.5g packet)	16.7g	1 tbsp. + ⅓ tsp.
2.5g (½ of a 5g packet)	25g	1 tbsp. + 2 tsp.
2.875g (¼ of an 11.5g packet)	28.8g	2 tbsp.
3.3g (⅓ of a 5g packet)	33g	2 tbsp. + 1 tsp.
5.75g (½ of an 11.5g packet)	57.5g	¼ c.
7.67g (⅔ of an 11.5g packet)	76.7g	⅓ c.

REHYDRATING YEAST with A REHYDRATION NUTRIENT

Weight of yeast	Weight of Go-Ferm required	Approximate volume of Go-Ferm	Weight of water required	Approximate volume of water
1.25g (¼ of a 5g packet)	1.56g	½ tsp.	31g	2 tbsp.
1.67g (¼ of an 11.5g packet)	2.1g	⅔ tsp.	42g	2 tbsp. + 2½ tsp.
2.5g (½ of a 5g packet)	3.1g	1 tsp.	62g	¼ c.
2.875g (¼ of an 11.5g packet)	3.6g	1 heaping tsp.	72g	¼ c. + 1 tbsp.
3.3g (⅓ of a 5g packet)	4.1g	1⅓ tsp.	82.5g	⅓ c.
5.75g (½ of an 11.5g packet)	7.2g	2 heaping tsp.	144g	½ c. + 2 tbsp.
7.67g (⅔ of an 11.5g packet)	9.6g	1 heaping tbsp.	192g	¾ c. + 1 tbsp.

1. Allow your yeast packet to come to room temperature.
2. Heat water in a microwave or on a burner to 104°F.
3. Place a sterile, heat-resistant, microwaveable container on your scale and zero it out.
4. Add water to the container until the scale reads twenty times the weight of the Go-Ferm you will be using. (See chart above.)
5. Stir in the Go-Ferm with a sanitized spoon.
6. Sprinkle the yeast evenly on top, avoiding clumps.
7. Cover with plastic wrap and wait 15 to 30 minutes.
8. Gently stir with a sanitized spoon.
9. Yeast is ready to pitch once the temperature drops to the desired yeast pitching/fermentation temperature. (It should not rehydrate for more than 30 minutes.)

Sugars and Sugar Sources (a.k.a. Yeast Food)

Sugar is a sweet, crystalline carbohydrate composed of carbon and hydrogen. The sugars we're concerned with in brewing are generally either monosaccharides, which are simple structures, such as glucose and fructose; or disaccharides, slightly more complex structures, such as sucrose and maltose. Disaccharides are made up of monosaccharides, and yeast will break them down into those monosaccharides before consuming them.

The simplest sugars to use in brewing are the ones that you purchase ready-to-use. These range from highly refined white sugars to less refined cane sugars such as panela to syrups such as maple or honey. That said, fruit will be a key source of sugar for many of the fermentations in this book, and in the beer section, we'll extract sugar from malted barley and wheat using a process called mashing. Here's a quick overview of the various sugars we'll encounter.

Agave syrup. Agave syrup is made from agave juice that is heated, filtered, and concentrated into a syrup. It is composed of fructose and glucose and is therefore highly fermentable. It's available in raw, light, amber, and dark varieties, and the nutritional value will vary as will the aroma, flavor, and color contribution to the finished beverage.

Brown sugar. A sucrose sugar with a brown color due to the presence of molasses, brown sugar can be made with unrefined, partially refined, or refined (white) sugar. It's usually refined from sugarcane but can also come from sugar beets. There are many different types of brown sugars, including whole cane sugar, demerara, turbinado, muscovado, panela, rapadura, and piloncillo. Brown sugars are generally easy to source and can be quite inexpensive. They may contribute some aroma and flavor to the finished beverage and typically contain some nutrients that the yeast can use.

Demerara. Demerara (turbinado) is a type of brown sugar made by crystallizing sugarcane juice. Like other brown sugars, it is less processed than white sugar and therefore retains some molasses. It is amber in color, may contribute to the aroma and flavor of the finished beverage, and contains some nutrients for the yeast. Demerara is interchangeable with turbinado for our purposes.

13

Corn sugar. Corn sugar (dextrose) is highly processed sugar made up of glucose. It's 100 percent fermentable, contributes little color or flavor to the finished beverage, and provides few to no nutrients to the yeast. It's often used to lighten the body of beers and to bottle-condition fermented beverages. (See page 26.)

Fruit. The sugar in fruit is primarily fructose. Fruit may add a significant amount of fermentable sugar along with aroma, flavor, and nutrients, depending on the type of fruit and how it is used. However, fresh fruit also contains a lot of water by weight. Fermented beverages may be made of 100 percent fruit juice or may use a combination of whole fruit and juice to add aroma and flavor. Fruit may be used fresh, dried, freeze-dried, pulped, frozen, or in juice form.

Honey. A sugar-packed syrup created by bees from flower nectar, honey is mostly composed of glucose and fructose and is highly fermentable. Honey comes in a wide variety of flavors, depending on the type of plant whose nectar the bee collects. Honey adds fermentable sugar to a beverage and may also add significant aroma and flavor, depending on the variety of honey used.

Jaggery. Jaggery is one of the less refined sugars, and it can be made from sugarcane, palm, date palm, or coconut palm. Jaggery is composed primarily of sucrose with up to 20 percent invert sugar. As it is unrefined, it contains some nutrients for the yeast and may contribute some aroma, flavor, and color to the finished beverage. It may be found in international markets or aisles, particularly those specializing in goods from India and nearby Southeast Asian countries.

Malted grains. Malting is a process in which grains are partially germinated and dried with hot air, preparing them for the brewing process. Malted grains contain starches as well as enzymes that will convert these starches to sugars in the right conditions. Malted grains primarily add sugar in the form of maltose but may also add maltotriose, glucose, sucrose, fructose, or unfermentable dextrins. Malted grains contribute not only sugar but also aroma, flavor, and nutrients to your beverage.

Maltose. Maltose is a disaccharide made up of two glucose molecules. It is the primary sugar produced in mashing grain to make beer.

Maple syrup. Maple syrup is a sweet syrup created from the sap of red, black, or sugar maple trees. The syrup is made by boiling freshly collected sap to lower the moisture content through evaporation. Maple syrup comes in several grades, depending on its color. It is highly fermentable and may contribute aroma, flavor, and color to the finished beverage, varying with the grade of the syrup.

Molasses. Also known as black treacle, molasses is usually made by boiling sugar syrup, either from sugarcane or sugar beets. However, it can also be derived from sorghum or a variety of fruits, as pomegranate molasses is. The type of molasses is determined by the number of times the syrup is boiled or the length of the boil. Molasses provides some nutrients to the yeast and affects the aroma, flavor, and color of the finished beverage.

Muscovado. Also known as Barbados sugar or molasses sugar, muscovado is a dark brown, minimally refined cane sugar that retains a high percentage of molasses. It can contribute significantly to the aroma, flavor, and color of the finished beverage and contains some nutrients for the yeast.

Panela. An unrefined cane sugar produced by boiling and evaporating sugarcane juice, panela is a solid form of sucrose that is amber to dark brown in color. As it is less refined, it will contribute aroma, flavor, and color to the finished beverage as well as provide some nutrients to the yeast. Panela is produced in Latin and Central America and may be found in that section of your local grocery store or in international markets. It is inexpensive and is one of my favorite sugars to ferment. You may also find it under the names piloncillo or rapadura.

White granulated sugar (sucrose). Also known as table sugar, cane sugar, or beet sugar, white sugar is highly refined and composed of sucrose, a disaccharide comprising glucose and fructose. Around 80 percent of table sugar is refined from sugarcane with the remaining 20 percent from sugar beets. Sugar may also be obtained from the sugar maple, date palm, and sorghum, but this is much less common. Table sugar is 100 percent fermentable, meaning that all of it can be consumed by the yeast and converted to carbon dioxide and alcohol. White sugar is readily available and inexpensive, contributes very little to no aroma or flavor to the finished beverage, and is devoid of nutrients for the yeast.

Nutrients

Yeast require an array of nutrients, including nitrogen, amino acids, fatty acids, sterols, minerals, and vitamins, in order to properly ferment. In beer brewing the liquid substrate called wort typically contains the required nutrients, but many sugar, honey, and fruit-based substrates do not. There are several different nutrient mixes available to home fermenters, but I recommend beer yeast nutrient, which is readily available from homebrew supply stores, for all of the fast-fermentation recipes in this book. See page 12 for the recommended process and amount to use.

EQUIPMENT

Basic Brewing Equipment

Fermentation vessels (jugs, jars, buckets). All of the recipes in this book are one-gallon batches except the beer recipes, which are two-gallon batches. For one-gallon batches, I recommend using a one-gallon glass jug or wide-mouth glass jar with a plastic lid. I choose the wide-mouth jar if I'm fermenting anything with fruits or other chunky additives that would be difficult to get in and out of a narrow-neck container. Both types are available at homebrewing supply shops and from online vendors.

You can also find jugs in recycling bins, at yard sales, at flea markets, and prefilled at liquor and grocery stores. (Just drink the wine or juice that comes in them first!) One-gallon jugs will typically take a No. 5.5 or No. 6 stopper, and the plastic lids of wide-mouth jars can be cut or drilled and fitted with a grommet to accept an airlock. An inexpensive and readily available alternative is to use a one-gallon clear plastic jug of spring water (the crystal-clear type, not the semitranslucent variety). These usually cost around a dollar at your local grocery, drug, or discount store and are easy to adapt for fermentation by either drilling or cutting a hole in the lid to fit an airlock grommet or by adding a medium-size stopper. And the water inside is perfect for using in your fermentations. I recommend removing just enough water to allow space for your fermentables; there is no need to remove all of the water, sanitize, and add water back in.

For two-gallon batches, I recommend two-gallon food-grade buckets, which can

as well as brewing. One of my favorites is a wide-neck funnel made of silicone that collapses and has a removable strainer insert in the bottom. I also find that having several sizes of narrow-neck funnels comes in handy. Funnels can be purchased at discount, kitchen supply, and variety stores.

Auto-siphon, racking cane, tubing, and bottling wand. Pictured at left, the auto-siphon, racking cane, and tubing are used to transfer, or rack, your liquid from one container to another. An auto-siphon and racking cane allow you to draw your liquid up and through the attached tubing with minimal air exposure. They're easy to use and extremely convenient, and they come in a variety of sizes, including a mini auto-siphon and racking cane set that works perfectly for one-gallon batches. Tubing is used to transfer beer to the bottling bucket and also to transfer many of the other beverages in this book directly into bottles with a bottling wand.

be purchased at a local homebrewing or a restaurant supply store. You can also split your two-gallon batch of beer into two one-gallon glass jugs or jars if you'd like.

Funnels. You probably already have the funnels that you'll need for the recipes in this book in your kitchen. I recommend one narrow-neck and one wide-neck plastic, silicone, or stainless-steel funnel. I keep a variety of kitchen funnels on hand, as they are inexpensive and useful for cooking

Strainers and sieves. I use a variety of plastic strainers that I've found at local dollar stores. They usually come prepackaged in sets of three different sizes. I have a set that is all plastic mesh and another that has plastic sides and mesh bottoms; both types are useful. Mesh tea infusers also come in handy.

Bungs and stoppers. Drilled rubber or silicone stoppers are used to hold an airlock on the glass jugs. Glass jugs typically take a No. 5.5 or No. 6 stopper; wider-mouth plastic jugs might take a slightly larger one.

Airlocks. Airlocks prevent air, wild bacteria, and yeast from getting into your fermenting beverage while allowing carbon dioxide produced by the yeast to escape. Airlocks come in two different varieties: a three-piece, straight-sided type and a single-piece, S-shaped type. Both work just fine.

Hydrometers. Hydrometers allow brewers to measure the sugar content of their wort or substrate, determine when the fermentation is over, and calculate the alcoholic strength of their beverage. To take a reading, you simply place the hollow glass tube into a cylinder filled with your liquid and read it according to the gradations on the paper inside the glass. (See the sidebar for complete instructions.)

The hydrometer measures the specific gravity of your beverage, which is its density in relation to water. The more sugar in your beverage, the higher the specific gravity—as the yeast consumes the sugar and produces alcohol, the gravity will drop, as alcohol is less dense than sugar.

GETTING STARTED

TAKING A GRAVITY READING USING A HYDROMETER

You must maintain sanitary practices when taking hydrometer readings. I use a clean, sanitized, stainless-steel baster to collect liquid for gravity readings. Collect the liquid (optimally at 60°F) with the sanitized baster and transfer to the hydrometer tube. Add the hydrometer to the tube gently so it doesn't hit the bottom of the tube hard; you don't want to dislodge the paper inside or break the hydrometer. Place the tube of liquid on a level surface, gently spin the hydrometer, and allow it to come to a rest. It should be floating independently and not sticking to the side of the tube. If it sticks, give it another gentle spin. Read the number in the specific gravity column where the liquid crosses the marking on your hydrometer and make a note of it in your brewing notebook or software. If you are taking a reading after fermentation, note that dissolved CO_2 can affect the hydrometer reading. I stir or shake my postfermentation samples vigorously to degas them before taking a reading.

You'll take gravity readings at least twice when brewing—after you finish brewing but before you pitch your yeast and then again at the end of your fermentation. (You might also take one or two along the way to see how your fermentation is faring.) The two readings can be entered into an online calculator or hand-calculated to find your alcohol by volume (ABV). Most hydrometers are calibrated for 60°F, although some are calibrated for 68°F; this information is printed on the paper that comes inside your hydrometer. If you are measuring liquid at a different temperature than your hydrometer is calibrated for, you must account for this in your calculations. Online ABV calculators help you do this by requesting the temperatures your readings were taken at.

Brew pot. I use a five-gallon stainless-steel pot for the two-gallon beer batches in this book. You may also use an enameled pot, but aluminum is not recommended.

Teakettle. I recommend a basic teakettle for quickly boiling water for some of the recipes in this book. You may also use a small saucepan if you don't own a kettle. Electric or stovetop kettles are ridiculously fast and convenient for heating, boiling, and pouring water to prepare teas and other ingredients for infusion. I recommend the variety that whistles. When heating water to below boiling temperatures, I stick the probe of my wired thermometer down the spout and set the alarm to my desired temperature.

Grommets. Rubber grommets allow you to convert any plastic lid to a fermentation lid. Simply trace the inside of the grommet onto your lid with a permanent marker and create a hole using a craft knife or a drill. (I recommend a quick sanding to smooth the edges if you use a craft knife.) Insert your grommet and your airlock, and you are ready to ferment. Airlock-size grommets can be purchased from homebrewing supply stores.

Cleanser. Though you can use dish soap and water to clean most of your equipment, an oxygenating powdered cleanser is excellent for removing yeast remnants and other hard-to-remove gunk from your fermenting equipment. I buy a brand readily available at my local market, but homebrew stores carry similar products that are made for cleaning brewing equipment. Most require hot water to dissolve fully.

Sanitizer. Sanitation is key to clean fermentations. Homebrewing stores carry sanitizers specifically made for brewing; I recommend a no-rinse foaming sanitizer, but there are others available that work just as well. I don't recommend using bleach, as it is difficult to rinse fully, and any left behind may give your beverage an off-flavor. On brew days, I clean all of my materials and then fill two containers with sanitizing solution: a wide-mouth pint glass jar and a large plastic tub. I place smaller items (such as the thermometer, scissors, and teaspoon) in the glass jar and larger items (funnels, strainers, and lids) in the tub. I then fill my

21

fermenting jars and jugs with sanitizer. I also keep a small spray bottle full of sanitizer solution for spot-sanitizing.

Thermometers. I use two thermometers for brewing: a water-resistant, instant-read, digital pocket thermometer and a cooking thermometer with a detachable wire probe and temperature alarms. Almost any kitchen thermometer will do, though, so start with what you have. If you decide to purchase a new thermometer, I recommend the water-resistant, quick-read, digital type. It doesn't need to be a fancy, top-of-the line version—a basic one will do. A wire-probed thermometer that has temperature-triggered alarms is very handy when mashing grain for beers and malt sodas as well as heating water to a specific temperature.

Brew bag. For small-batch brewing, a variety of brew bags may be used. Large hop bags and paint strainer bags are two options to start. You're looking for something large enough to fit your brew pot into with fabric woven tight enough to hold your crushed grain yet loose enough to let it drain. Many homebrewing supply shops sell bags specifically made for brewing, and there are online suppliers as well. If you sew or know someone who does, you can easily make your own. I structure mine in a bucket shape, with a circular bottom and straight sides. I use a synthetic fabric for the body and stitch on a cotton collar for sturdiness. Again, you'll want to make the bag large enough to fit your brew pot into with a fabric tight

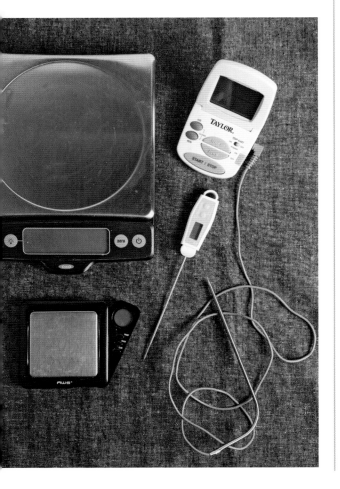

enough to hold your crushed grain yet loose enough to let it drain. If you want to get fancy, you can even stitch on handles and add a casing and drawstring.

Spoons. A large, long-handled, stainless-steel brew spoon is recommended for the beer chapter. The stainless spoons that you already use for cooking and dining are all that's needed for the other recipes.

Scale. At least one digital scale is essential for weighing out the ingredients that we will be using in this book. I have two for brewing: a digital kitchen scale for measuring out larger quantities of ingredients, such as honey, and a small digital pocket scale for measuring out smaller quantities of ingredients such as herbs, spices, and hops. The pocket scale I use weighs up to one kilogram in tenth-gram increments and also measures in ounces.

Heat-tolerant pitcher. You'll need a heat-tolerant pitcher that holds four or more cups for making teas and infusions. You can use a nonreactive metal or glass saucepan, but a container with a pouring spout is ideal. I keep several heat-tolerant glass pitchers on hand but find that I use the two-cup and four-cup sizes the most.

Bottles and caps. I have traditionally used glass bottles for beer and short meads but have recently begun using plastic bottles for all of the fermentations that I don't keg. Plastic bottles are easy to use, as they have screw caps, withhold a high degree of pressure from carbonation, and are lighter to transport. I purchase five-hundred-milliliter brown polyethylene terephthalate (PET) bottles by the case at my local homebrew store. Glass bottles come in a variety of shapes and sizes; you can save up beer bottles at home, ask a local bar to save bottles for you, or purchase new bottles at a homebrew supply shop. Look for bottles without screw tops and with standard-size openings. You will need a capper and fresh caps to go with your bottles. Handheld cappers are the least expensive and easiest type to use. A note of caution if you go with used bottles: some international beers come in bottles with a different-diameter opening and have an irregular neck, requiring a different-size cap and floor-type capper. Flip-top bottles, also called EZ Cap bottles, do not require a capper and are more convenient but cost more than standard bottles. Use only flip-top bottles that are designed for carbonated beverages. Decorative flip-top bottles are available but are not designed to hold pressure. For all of the nonbeer fermentations in this book, I recommend plastic bottles, but flip-top glass bottles may also be used with caution.

Brewing notebook. A must. You'll want to keep track of your recipes, ingredient sources, variations, gravities, tasting notes, and so on. This could be digital or paper—whichever works best for you. I've been lax a few times over the years and have not written a recipe down, and I always regret it. Your brewing notebook doesn't need to be fancy, but you definitely want to keep all of your lovely fermentation experiments in one place for future reference. I encourage you to record tasting notes and future ideas as well as recipes in your notebook.

Optional but Recommended Equipment

Refractometer. A refractometer can be used to measure the specific gravity of your sugar solution. The advantage it has over a hydrometer is that it requires a much smaller sample size, usually only a few drops of liquid. This is terrific for small-batch fermenting. However, there are some disadvantages. Refractometers measure most accurately in degrees Brix, which must be converted to specific gravity. They need to be calibrated, and they don't accurately measure when alcohol is present, as in postfermentation readings; they're also designed for sucrose-based solutions, so readings need to be corrected for wort. Refractometers are definitely not necessary, but if you really get into small-batch, sugar-based fermentations, you might want to put one on your wish list.

pH meter or test strips. pH meters and test strips measure the acidity or alkalinity of a solution. This isn't a concern for the majority of the recipes in this book but is useful when making kombucha and water kefir. pH meters are more of an investment but cover a wide range of pH readings. If you'd like to use pH test strips, the type that measure in the lower range, under 5, are the most useful for kombucha and water kefir.

Kegging equipment. Kegging saves considerable time and hassle compared to bottling. It requires a larger up-front investment than bottling does, but kegging is inexpensive to maintain. A basic kegging setup includes a CO_2 tank, a regulator, gas and liquid line assemblies, and a keg. Not so long ago, the smallest kegs available to homebrewers were 5 gallons. That has changed recently, and homebrewers now have access to kegs as small as 1.75 gallons—the perfect size for the 2-gallon beer recipes in this book or a double batch of any of the 1-gallon recipes. Mini regulators are available, and small CO_2 tanks designed for paintball use may be used instead of a larger five- or ten-pound tank.

Carbonation caps are another option for small-batch brewers with the money for some kegging equipment. These are plastic caps that fit any standard screw-top soda bottle. The caps fit a standard ball-lock gas disconnect and allow you to force-carbonate almost any size soda bottle. There are other small-batch options available for serving your beer, including a system designed to fit on a standard fridge shelf. While I don't recommend investing in a kegging system when you first begin fermenting alcoholic beverages, I do think it's worth noting as more and more small-batch kegging options become available. If you find yourself pulled into the vortex of fast small-batch fermentations, consider adding a kegging setup. It's very rewarding to be able to offer guests a fresh draft pour of your latest boozy creation!

Travel Fermentation Equipment

One of the fun things about fast fermentations is that they can be made almost anywhere with very little equipment. If I am away for a week or more, I enjoy bringing along a travel fermentation kit:

- Dry yeast packets
- Yeast nutrient mix
- Airlocks
- Rubber grommets to fit airlocks
- Travel-size container of sanitizer

I seal everything inside a plastic bag and toss it in my luggage. I try to avoid exposing the yeast packets to extreme heat. I purchase one-gallon jugs of water, cut holes in the lids to fit the rubber grommets, and use these to ferment in. I subtract just enough water to allow enough space for the fermentables that I am adding. I use plastic soda or water bottles to bottle into. Travel brewing offers a nice chance to experiment and create something tasty even when you're away from home.

PACKAGING

All of the recipes in this book are designed to be carbonated beverages. As I discussed at the beginning of this chapter, yeast convert sugar into alcohol and carbon dioxide—we're going to capture some of that carbon dioxide in order to add bubbles to our beverages. This will be done in two different ways, depending on the type of beverage.

For the beers, we are going to wait until the yeast have finished their primary fermentation. We'll then add a priming sugar to our beer and bottle, a step called bottle conditioning. This additional sugar will rouse the yeast and provide them with more fuel for creating carbon dioxide. Since the liquid is in a closed container, the CO_2 will remain in the bottle. Bottle conditioning does pose a risk of overcarbonating; you must measure your priming sugar accurately for the beers and bottle at proper gravity and/or drink quickly for the others in order to prevent gushing—or worse, exploding—bottles. This is why I recommend glass bottles for the beers and plastic for the other beverages, though flip-top glass may be used with great care.

For all of the other beverages in this book, we'll be bottling before the primary fermentation has fully finished. We'll be taking advantage of the sugar remaining at this stage and providing a closed environment to trap the CO_2 and carbonate our beverages. Every nonbeer beverage in this book (and the Bia Hoi and Pennsylvania Swankey in the beer chapter) is designed to be fermented quickly and enjoyed fresh. These are lively flavored beverages that beg to be consumed quickly.

Why the difference between the beverages? Beer is created by fermenting wort made from malted grains. This wort contains complex sugars that aren't fermentable by the yeast, so it leaves some residual sugars and body. However, the simple sugars used for nonbeer fermenting are often 100 percent fermentable, meaning that the yeast will chew through everything, leaving no residual sugar. Some of sugar-based beverages may still retain perceived sweetness even when they have no sugar left, but this is usually due to other flavor compounds that remain from the raw ingredients or that developed during the fermentation. By bottling the nonbeer beverages before they finish fermenting, we are not only harnessing the natural CO_2 that is being produced; we are also retaining some sugar and body that we would lose by allowing them to completely finish their fermentations.

There are additives used by professional cider, mead, and wine makers to arrest fermentation, as well as methods of back-sweetening after fermentation, but we won't use those techniques in this book. Note that kegged beer and many commercial bottled beers are not naturally conditioned, but force-carbonated with CO_2. These beers are often filtered before packaging as well. However, since all of the beverages in this book will be naturally carbonated, you'll find a layer of yeast at the bottom of the bottle—this is normal, natural, and completely acceptable. Just pour slowly and leave as much yeast as possible in the bottle when you serve.

Bottling Beer

In this book the goal is to bottle all of the beers after they have reached terminal gravity. For most of the lower-alcohol beer recipes in this book, this will likely happen after five to seven days. It's a good idea to give them some extra time to settle out and condition before bottling, though. I recommend taking a gravity reading seven days after bottling. (See the sidebar on page 20.) Take another reading a couple of days later and then one last reading a day or two after that. If your gravity readings are near the expected final gravity for your beer and are the same over the three readings, your beer has reached terminal gravity. If you have space in your refrigerator, I recommend chilling the beer for a day or two before bottling. This will encourage extra yeast, protein, and tannins to settle out. When you're ready to bottle, allow your beer to warm to room temperature again before bottling.

Materials

- Cleaning and sanitizing equipment (see pages 21–22)
- Corn or cane sugar (see page 15)
- Bottling bucket
- Auto-siphon, racking cane, and tubing
- Spring-tip bottle filler
- Stainless-steel long-handled spoon
- Small saucepan
- Bottles and caps
- Capper

Instructions

1. Clean and sanitize all of your materials and equipment: bottling bucket, racking equipment, bottles, and bottle caps.

2. Prepare your priming sugar solution. You can use almost any type of sugar for priming, but corn sugar and cane sugar are easy and add no additional flavor. You'll prepare your sugar solution by boiling the sugar in ¾ cup of water for 10 minutes. See the chart at bottom left for the recommended priming sugar amounts for 2 gallons of beer. Adjust up or down according to your batch size (and note that there are online calculators you can use as well).

    An alternative to priming sugar is to use carbonation drops or tabs. These are added directly to each bottle. There are several types on the market; some are used 1 per 12-ounce bottle, while others are used 3 to 5 per 12-ounce bottle. The advantage of the latter is that it allows you to choose your level of carbonation. They also minimize the risk of overcarbonating and allow you to eliminate the need for a bottling bucket.

3. Cover priming solution (plastic wrap works fine here) and chill it in an ice bath until it's within 5°F of your beer temperature.

4. Once your priming solution has cooled, add it to your sanitized bottling bucket.

5. Transfer your beer to the bottling bucket. You want to minimize agitation and oxygenation as much as possible, and racking with an auto-siphon, cane, and tubing is ideal. If you don't have these, I recommend pouring from your fermentation vessel very slowly against the wall of your bottling bucket to reduce splashing.

Desired Carbonation	Amount of Corn Sugar (Dextrose)	Amount of Cane Sugar (Sucrose)
Low	1 oz.	0.9 oz.
Medium	1.8 oz.	1.6 oz.
High	3 oz.	2.7 oz.

29

6. Gently stir with a sanitized spoon to thoroughly mix the solution.

7. Lift your bottling bucket up onto a counter. Attach tubing that is long enough to reach your bottling area and the bottle-filler tip. Fill the bottles with beer.

8. Cap the bottles and store in a dark location at room temperature. Your beer should be carbonated and ready to drink in around 1½ to 2 weeks.

Bottling Everything Else

You will bottle most of the beverages in this book before they reach terminal gravity. Depending on the level of sweetness and carbonation that you desire, you may wish to bottle when your beverage reaches a specific gravity of 1.002 to 1.008. The higher the gravity, the more active the fermentation is and the faster your bottles will carbonate (and need to be drunk). I recommend bottling around 1.004 to 1.006 for most of the beverages. You can adjust as needed, depending on your preferred sweetness and carbonation level. If your beverages ferment out faster than you expected, or if you let them go a little too long and they end up at a lower gravity, you can bottle with carbonation tabs. (See page 28.) Use the type that allows you to choose from three to five tabs for a twelve-ounce bottle. The beverage will be drier than you might want, but at least it will be carbonated!

I highly recommend plastic bottles for all of these beverages, as plastic bottles tolerate a much higher amount of pressure and won't break or explode under normal amounts of pressure. What's more, you can tell when their contents are carbonated by squeezing the sides of the bottles. If you would like to use glass, I recommend flip-top bottles over hand-capped bottles. You can release pressure with a flip-top bottle and re-cap it easily. In cases of extreme carbonation, the flip-top tends to give before the bottle breaks—but it is still dangerous, since you can't check on carbonation in a glass bottle as you can with plastic. If you do choose to bottle in glass, use one plastic bottle in every batch. That way, you can tell when your bottles are carbonated; the plastic bottle will have little give when ready—and you'll know when to refrigerate all of your bottles. Chilling slows fermentation greatly but will not stop it, so do drink the bottles sooner rather than later.

Chilling before bottling is recommended for many of these beverages, if you have room in your refrigerator. Chilling for a day before bottling will encourage fruit, hops, and other materials to drop to the bottom, making it easier to bottle the liquid. Bring the beverage back up to room temperature before bottling.

Materials

- Cleaning and sanitizing equipment (see pages 21–22)
- Auto-siphon, racking cane, and tubing or funnel, strainer and tubing
- Bottles and caps
- Capper

Instructions

1. Clean and sanitize all bottling equipment.
2. Fill the bottles. The most efficient way to fill bottles is to use an auto-siphon, racking cane, and tubing with a spring-tip bottle filler attached. If you don't have these or if the neck of the jug is too narrow for the auto-siphon, use a funnel with plastic tubing attached. The plastic tubing should end just above the bottom of your bottles. Very gently pour the beverage into the funnel, minimizing splashing. Use a strainer if the beverage contains fruit, hops, or other particulates.
3. Cap the bottles and store in a dark location at room temperature for a day or two, until the bottles do not have any give.
4. Refrigerate and drink within a week or so. Many of the beverages will stabilize at cooler temperatures and last for months but may lose aroma, flavor, and liveliness along the way.

2

BRISK BEER

BRISK BEER? That probably sounds like an oxymoron to some of you. While making beer from scratch does require a longer brew day and more time in the fermenter than most of the other beverages in this book, it is possible to speed up the process without sacrificing deliciousness. Here's how:

1. We'll shave time off of the brew day by using a technique called Brew in a Bag (BIAB). A BIAB system allows you to brew an all-grain beer in less time, both in brewing and cleanup, and with fewer pieces of equipment.

2. We'll also save time on brew day by brewing small batches, about two gallons in size. This saves time when you're heating water for the mash and wort for the boil.

3. We'll save time during fermentation by brewing beers that are low in alcohol, or sessionable.

If you've never brewed beer before, this chapter will introduce you to the ingredients and process and provide some simple recipes to get you started. I've also included a couple of more creative recipes for those of you who already homebrew and are interested in trying a new technique or two. If you get hooked on homebrewing and would like to explore it further than this chapter, I recommend joining a local homebrew club as well as the American Homebrewers Association. While there's a wealth of good information on the Internet, nothing beats a solid homebrewing book. I recommend *How to Brew* by John Palmer and *The Complete Joy of Homebrewing* by Charlie Papazian.

BREW in a BAG

MY CRAZY FREE FALL down the rabbit hole of brewing, my mad love for fermentation—it all began with beer. My first sip of hoppy amber ale in college won me over to beer drinking. However, it wasn't until years later that I began brewing. I blame the lag time on 7:15 a.m. chemistry labs, for which our grade was based largely on the percent yield of the product of that morning's chemical reaction. This was a little too close to calculating hop extraction, malt extraction, and attenuation for me. What if my beer wasn't hoppy enough or had too little alcohol? I enjoyed beer too much to worry about whether I could ace brewing or not.

Over the years that followed, those barriers broke down as my love of beer grew. Once I was given a homebrew kit, I knew it was time. I bought my ingredients at the only store with brewing supplies that we had in NYC in those years. It was actually a hydroponics store with a back corner of brewing supplies! Most customers paid with rolls of cash, and no one could answer my brewing questions.

Yet my first extract beer, a basic pale ale, turned out pretty well. It wasn't perfect, of course. But it was good enough that the manager of my local craft beer bottle shop gave it a thumbs-up and suggested I join a local homebrew club. There were only two

in NYC at the time, and I chose the one that met the soonest, which turned out to be the Malted Barley Appreciation Society. I don't remember who spoke at that meeting, but what I do remember is that Alex Hall, the president at the time, announced that the New York City Homebrewers Guild was hosting classes to prepare for the Beer Judge Certification Program (BJCP) exam in June. It was the first time in eight years that exam would be given in NYC. I was in. Those preparatory classes not only taught me a great deal about brewing, they opened a whole new world for me.

I quickly moved from extract brewing to partial-mash and then all-grain brewing,

and I found myself joyfully brewing five-gallon batches in my shared Brooklyn backyard. However, I wasn't physically strong enough to move the brew kettle by myself after sparging and had to rely on a neighbor or brewing partner to help. A little research led me to the Brew in a Bag method, where the entire brewing process is conducted in the brew kettle. Not only could I brew by myself, the BIAB method saved time and required less cleanup. And my beers were just as good, if not better, using BIAB instead of my traditional all-grain setup. I've been brewing using the BIAB method ever since.

The other advantage of BIAB is that it works particularly well for smaller batches. I brew batches ranging from one to five gallons using the BIAB method. A two-gallon batch size is what I'll use as a basis for the recipes in this book; it's fast and will yield you around twenty bottles or fit perfectly in the newer two-gallon kegs available to homebrewers. However, if you are already an all-grain brewer with a five-gallon setup, the recipes will scale up just fine.

Let's first take a look at the brewing process, and then move on to a BIAB brew day.

THE BREWING PROCESS

Cleaning and Sanitizing

Cleaning and sanitizing may sound like the same thing, but they're different and equally important parts of making good beer. Cleaning is what you'd expect: making sure your brewing materials are free of dirt and debris. I use an oxygenated powder cleanser mixed with very hot water, then rinse my equipment clean.

For equipment that touches the wort before or during the boil, cleaning is good enough. However, everything that comes into contact with your wort after the boil must be sanitized as well. I use a foaming no-rinse liquid sanitizer in the following way: I mix up enough sanitizer to fill a three- to four-gallon plastic tub and a wide-mouth pint glass jar. I place all of the equipment that I will be using after I begin my boil into these containers. My instant-read thermometer and scissors go into the glass jar, and my funnel, strainer, siphoning equipment, brew spoon, airlock, and stopper go into the plastic tub. My yeast container goes into whichever container it fits into, depending on the yeast packaging. A spray bottle of premixed sanitizing solution is also handy. (Remember to keep your hands clean on brew day as well!)

Note: As mentioned in Chapter 1, I don't recommend using bleach for sanitization. It's nearly impossible to rinse away fully and can lead to unpleasant aromas and flavors in your finished beer.

Mashing

Mashing is the process during which the starches in the grain are broken down into sugars that dissolve into solution. This solution, called wort, will provide the food that the yeast will convert to alcohol and carbon dioxide. The enzymes that were developed in the grain during the malting process are activated in certain temperature ranges; when active, the enzymes break down the starch within the grain to simple sugars. As brewers, we are concerned with two specific enzymes, alpha amylase and beta amylase. These enzymes work together in the mash to produce sugars that are fermentable by the yeast.

A mash temperature range of 152°F to 154°F is used for the majority of the recipes in this book, as it activates both of the appropriate enzymes. Mashing your malt

at this temperature range for an hour produces a wort that will give the yeast plenty of sugar to munch on. If you mash at a temperature a few degrees lower than 152°F, you'll get a more fermentable beer, meaning that there will be more sugar for your yeast to convert—in other words, your beer may end up drier and lighter in body. If you mash a few degrees higher than 154°F, there will be less sugar that your yeast can eat and you'll get a sweeter beer with more body. The enzymes are denatured around 170°F, meaning they won't convert starches to sugars above that temperature. This is called the mash-out temperature.

This process can be intimidating to new brewers, but it's really very simple

EFFICIENCY

Efficiency broadly refers to the amount of sugary wort that you are getting out of the grain with your brewing system. Each type of grain can contribute a specific amount of sugar, depending on malting, kilning, moisture content, milling, and other factors. The percentage of the sugar that you obtain from mashing the grain and collecting the wort is the efficiency of your brewing system. This isn't an exact calculation in homebrewing—we're not measuring with lab equipment, after all—but it's a good way to estimate the gravity of your wort and the alcohol you can expect after fermentation, and it can help you build recipes.

Efficiency can be calculated two different ways, using either preboil or postboil wort volume. The recipes in this book are calculated using 75 percent efficiency, assuming that we are collecting 2.5 gallons of wort after draining our grain bag and ending up with 2 gallons of wort after boil. You might end up with a slightly different extraction rate, meaning that you end up with a lower or higher original gravity than the recipe states. This can be due to differences in mash temperature, water pH, grain volume and straining

practice, boil rate, and the like. This is perfectly fine; you'll just end up with a slightly different ABV for your beer. If your original gravity is a lot lower than expected, you can add dry or liquid malt extract at the end of your boil. A half pound of liquid malt extract (LME) added to two gallons of wort will raise your gravity by around nine points. A half pound of dry malt extract (DME) added to two gallons of wort will raise your gravity by around ten points. For example, if you are striving for an original gravity of 1.045 and you end up with 1.035, you can add a half pound of DME to bring your wort to the desired gravity. Conversely, if you end up with a higher gravity than desired, you can dilute with filtered water at the end of the boil. If you find that you are under- or overshooting gravity consistently, this just means that you have a different efficiency than the recipe and you'll need to alter the amount of grain that you're using. This might sound complicated, but it's very easy when using brewing software. Once you've brewed a few batches, you'll have a better sense of the efficiency of your system and how to reach the desired gravity of your beer.

once you get the hang of it. Bottom line: shoot for a mash temperature between 152°F and 154°F and keep it there for an hour. It's okay if you're a couple of degrees off, but don't stray too far.

Draining

Lautering and sparging are, respectively, the processes of separating your grains from the wort and then rinsing them to obtain maximum sugar extraction. Traditional lautering and sparging require additional time and vessels, but the BIAB method skips this step, shaving about an hour off your brew day. Since the grains are enclosed in a cloth bag, removing this bag of grain from the brew kettle separates them from the wort. Some BIAB brewers do conduct a partial sparge, either by dunking the grain bag in a small pot of water or by pouring a small amount of water over the grain bag. This can boost your sugar extraction slightly. I only dunk-sparge when brewing beers that will ferment out to below 3 percent ABV, in which case every bit of sugar counts!

Boiling

Boiling not only sanitizes the wort, killing any existing yeast and bacteria, it also activates the hops (called isomerization),

coagulates undesirable proteins, evaporates unwanted compounds, and condenses the wort to target gravity. Boiling may be conducted for various amounts of time, but the recipes in this book generally require boiling the wort for an hour. You want a rolling boil in order to evaporate unwanted compounds and reach the target gravity. If you are able to obtain only a simmer on

39

the stovetop, you might want to invest in a wider kettle that can fit over two burners or use an electric heat stick. You can find DIY plans online to make your own heat stick or buy a premade one. In either case, be safe: follow the recommended electricity requirements for the heat stick and keep an eye on your boil.

Chilling

Cooling your beer quickly is very important. It reduces the risk of contamination, precipitates out unwanted proteins, and prevents the formation of unwanted compounds that may cause unpleasant aromas and flavors. Chilling may be done in an ice bath, but a wort chiller or counterflow chiller is even better. For chilling in an ice bath, use as large a bath as possible with a high ice-to-water ratio. Stir both the ice bath and your wort to maximize chilling, using a sanitized spoon for the wort and a second spoon for the ice bath. Adding rock salt to your ice bath will aid in chilling by lowering the freezing point of the water. Take care when stirring your ice bath, so that you do not splash it into your wort. If you are using a wort chiller and your tap water isn't cold enough (as is common in the summer), you can combine an ice bath with a wort chiller to achieve a lower wort temperature.

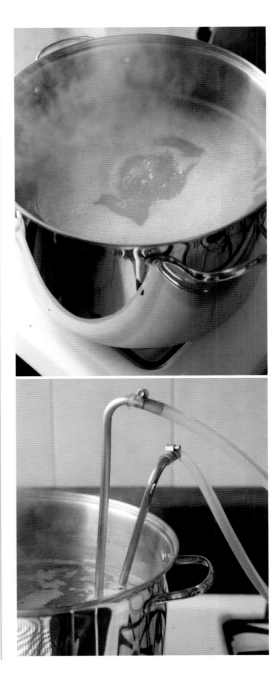

Fermenting

Once your wort is cool, you're ready to transfer it to your fermenter, oxygenate, and pitch the yeast. Once you pitch the yeast, it will feast on the sugars in the wort and turn them into alcohol and carbon dioxide. The yeast may also produce a number of aroma and flavor compounds, depending on the strain.

Temperature control is one of the most important factors in how the yeast will behave and, ultimately, how your beer will turn out. Each yeast strain has an optimal temperature range. It is important to keep the fermentation temperatures within this range, and it is important to keep the temperature constant. Very low temperatures may stall your fermentation, while high temperatures may cause the yeast to produce compounds that cause unwanted aromas and flavors. Temperature fluctuations may also stress the yeast. Keep in mind that fermentation creates heat, so you'll actually want to keep your fermentations slightly below your desired fermentation temperature—although this is not quite as problematic with smaller batches as the surface area to volume ratio is high and the heat does not build up. The most critical period for temperature control is in the first three days of fermentation.

There are many ways to control your fermentation temperature, depending on how much money, time, and space you wish to invest. Let's start with a few low-cost methods for keeping your fermentations cool:

- Take advantage of evaporative cooling by covering your bucket or jug with a dark, wet cotton T-shirt and pointing a fan at it. Rewet the shirt as it dries out.
- Keep your bucket or jug in a cold-water bath, known as a swamp cooler in the brewing community. Adding a couple of plastic bottles that have been filled with water and frozen will further help lower the water temperatures and keep it low. Stash a couple of extra frozen bottles in the freezer and swap them out as needed.
- You can keep smaller batches in a chest cooler, or build one with foam insulation board, and use plastic bottles full of frozen water to keep the temperature down.
- Buy a collapsible fabric fermentation chamber available from homebrewing suppliers. Again, this is something you cool with plastic bottles filled with water and frozen.

If you get hooked on brewing, you'll want to invest in a dedicated fermentation chamber, be it a dorm-size refrigerator or a chest freezer. Both of these can be fitted with an analog or digital temperature controller so you can dial in your fermentation temperatures precisely. Small refrigerators and chest freezers are relatively inexpensive and can be found used for cheap; check local classifieds boards. If you live in a university town, dorm fridges can often be had for free at the end of the school year. But what if your fermentation area is too cold? The simplest method is to construct an incubation chamber, either as a standalone or in an existing shelf. Use foam insulation board and provide a heat source in the form of either an incandescent light bulb or two or a heat grow mat fitted with a temperature regulator. If you use light bulbs for heat, you'll need to shield your fermentations from the light by using a thick, dark T-shirt or fabric or even a couple of black plastic bags. A converted refrigerator or chest freezer fitted with a temperature controller can also be used in colder months, of course.

INGREDIENTS

Malt

While water might make up the largest percentage of beer by volume, malts are the base with which all beers are made. Malts, in general, almost always refer to malted barley. After harvesting, raw barley must go through the malting process in order to prepare it for brewing.

In malting, the barley kernels are first sorted, cleaned, and then placed in steeping tanks, where they are submerged in water and drained several times over two to three days. This process, called steeping, increases the moisture content of the barley and triggers germination, the initial growth stage of the kernel. Once the barley reaches the desired moisture content, it is moved to the germination area. During germination, the kernels begin to sprout and send out visible rootlets. The processes taking place inside the kernel during this time are what's important to brewers: enzymes are developing, proteins and carbohydrates are breaking down, and starch reserves are becoming available. Once these are at the desired levels, germination is halted by a heating process called kilning, which dries the kernels; the level of heat, ventilation, and time determine the color, aroma, flavor, and diastatic power of the malted

barley. (Diastatic power is the enzymatic potency of the grain, or its ability to break down the starches in the kernel to simpler sugars during mashing.)

Malts like Pilsner and pale malt are kilned at low temperatures with more ventilation for a short period of time, resulting in pale color, light flavor, and high diastatic power. Malts like Munich and Vienna are dried at higher temperatures with less ventilation for longer periods of time, resulting in darker color, richer flavor, and medium diastatic power. Black and chocolate malts are kilned at even higher temperatures, resulting in very dark colors and little diastatic power, as

the enzymes are increasingly degraded at higher temperatures. Crystal malts, also called caramel malts, are unique in that they do not go through the initial drying phase and are kilned while wet, essentially creating a mini mash within each kernel, resulting in malts that contain sugar but have no diastatic power.

Today's brewers have a staggering variety of base malts, crystal malts, and darker roasted malts to choose from when creating their recipes. In addition to barley, other varieties of grain are used in brewing, including wheat, rye, oats, spelt, corn, rice, millet, and buckwheat. These malts may add different aroma and flavor characteristics as well as affect the body, head retention, and gluten content of the finished beer.

Malt must be crushed before it can be used to brew. When purchasing grains for use with BIAB, ask your homebrew store or supplier to crush them a bit finer for BIAB use. They can either adjust their mill to give you the finer grind required for

MALT CHART

Malt type	Examples	Steeped or mashed?	Lovibond Range*	Use in brewing
Base malts	Two-row, pale, wheat, Pilsner, smoked, Vienna, Munich	Must be mashed	1–10 L	Typically makes up the bulk of the malt bill in a recipe; adds the majority of the sugar as well as color, aroma, and flavor
Kilned, toasted, and roasted specialty malts	Brown, chocolate, roasted barley, black, coffee	May be steeped or mashed	5–800 L	Used as a small proportion of your malt bill to add color, aroma, and flavor
Crystal or caramel malts	CaraPils, honey, C15, C80, C120	May be steeped or mashed	3–150 L	Used as a small proportion of your malt bill to add color, aroma, flavor, and body
Unmalted and miscellaneous grains	Flaked barley, flaked wheat, millet, buckwheat	Must be mashed	1–300 L, though not applicable with flaked grains	Typically used in conjunction with base malts to add aroma and flavor or alter the body, mouthfeel, or protein content; may also be used in gluten-free beers

*Degrees Lovibond are the measurement that malters and brewers use to describe the color of malts and the finished beer. Color may also be expressed in Standard Reference Method (SRM). Lovibond degrees and SRM numbers correlate closely.

this method or crush the grains twice. If you own a mill, adjust two notches tighter than usual for a finer crush. An electric mill comes in handy for this job. I fitted my mill with a drill attachment once I went BIAB; hand-cranking a fine crush is a drag!

Hops

In brewing, hops refer to the female flowers, or cones, of the perennial climbing plant *Humulus lupulus*. Hops have many functions in beer. They add bittering balance and contribute aroma and flavor. They aid in protein coagulation and precipitation in the kettle. And they add head stability and help preserve the finished beer.

Just as with malt, some processing occurs with hops before brewers use them. While brewers can and do use hops wet, meaning fresh off the bine, this is possible only during a very small window of time after the hop harvest. So wet hop beers are often a celebration of the harvest, or a special beer released in fall (for US hops).

To turn fresh hops into a product that can be used year round, the hop cones are typically dried, processed, and packaged as quickly as possible after harvest.

Further processing before packaging means that dried hops may be purchased in several forms: whole, pellets, and even as an extract. (Pellets are hop flowers that have been ground and compressed into pellets, and extracts are just what they sound like: a liquid essence of the hop.)

There are pros and cons to each form. Some brewers prefer to use whole hops, as they believe these give the best hop character—and some like the filter bed that whole hops can provide in the kettle. However, pellet hops tend to be more widely available and in greater variety. They are easy for homebrew retailers to vacuum-seal and package. And they don't take up as much space in your freezer. For these reasons—primarily because they're the easiest to source—the recipes in this book call for pellet hops.

You can think about hops, and choose which to buy, according to their primary function. Hops used primarily for bittering, such as Warrior, tend to be affordable and available year round. Aroma hops, especially the popular varieties such as Mosaic and Citra, may cost more and be harder to find. Many hops can be used for both aroma and bittering. Although it's tempting to use the newest, trendiest hops, don't overlook the older, less expensive varieties—they make beautiful beers as well.

When you purchase hops, the package should always be marked with an AA percentage. This stands for alpha acids, and it helps you calculate the weight of hop pellets needed to achieve the desired International Bittering Units (IBUs) of the finished beer. The primary alpha acids in hops are humulone, cohumulone, and adhumulone. These are isomerized in the boil to iso-alpha acids, which contribute to the bitterness of the beer. The amount of bitterness in the beer is determined by the alpha acid percentage of the hops, types of alpha acids in the hops, amount of hops, and length of boil. Bittering hops are typically added at the beginning of the boil, although any hops added during the boil will contribute to the end IBUs of the beer.

Hops contain a variety of essential oils that contribute aroma and flavor to beer. Because the essential oils are highly volatile, aroma and flavor hops are usually added in the last twenty minutes of the boil, at the end of the boil, during wort chilling, or even postfermentation as dry hops.

Hops Chart. I've opted to classify hops (at right) by their aroma and flavor characteristics. This is a very general classification, as not only may hops display a spectrum of notes in beer, they may also vary

AROMA and FLAVOR of HOPS

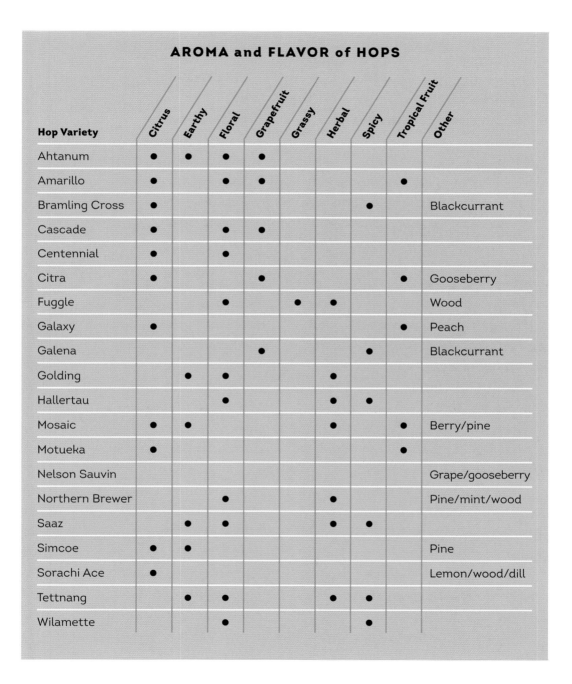

Hop Variety	Citrus	Earthy	Floral	Grapefruit	Grassy	Herbal	Spicy	Tropical Fruit	Other
Ahtanum	●	●	●	●					
Amarillo	●		●	●				●	
Bramling Cross	●						●		Blackcurrant
Cascade	●		●	●					
Centennial	●		●						
Citra	●			●				●	Gooseberry
Fuggle			●		●	●			Wood
Galaxy	●							●	Peach
Galena				●			●		Blackcurrant
Golding		●	●			●			
Hallertau			●			●	●		
Mosaic	●	●				●		●	Berry/pine
Motueka	●							●	
Nelson Sauvin									Grape/gooseberry
Northern Brewer			●			●			Pine/mint/wood
Saaz		●	●			●	●		
Simcoe	●	●							Pine
Sorachi Ace	●								Lemon/wood/dill
Tettnang		●	●			●	●		
Wilamette			●				●		

depending on where they are grown and other environmental conditions. Consult a hop directory or catalog or your homebrew supplier for a more complete list of hop varieties and their characteristics.

Yeast

Most homebrewers are concerned primarily with aroma and flavor contributions from yeast. However, there are many variables to consider when selecting a yeast strain. Each strain has different properties, including flocculation (ability of the yeast to clump together and fall out of suspension), attenuation (the percentage of sugars the yeast can consume), temperature range, and alcohol tolerance.

Brewing yeast may be purchased in wet or dry forms. Both forms have their pros and cons. Wet yeast is available in a much wider variety of strains than dry, but it is more expensive and has a shorter shelf life. Regardless of the type or variety of yeast that's used, temperature control is vital for home brewers and will bring out the best result in the finished beer—be sure to refer to temperature control information in the Fermenting section on pages 41 and 42.

Although dry yeast may be pitched directly into the beer, rehydration with a yeast rehydration nutrient will generally lead to better results. To rehydrate dry yeast with yeast rehydration nutrient:

1. Heat 1 cup water to 104°F in a sanitized container. I usually do this in the microwave.
2. Stir in 13 grams of yeast rehydration nutrient and sprinkle ½ packet of dry ale yeast on top.
3. Let stand for 20 minutes. Cool in an ice bath to desired pitching temperature, if necessary.

Yeast Chart. At right is a generalized yeast chart. There are a variety of strains that fit within each general category, each with different preferred temperature ranges and varying results in aromas, flavors, flocculation, attenuation, and alcohol tolerance. Refer to the manufacturer's website for more exacting descriptions for the particular yeast strain that you choose.

Water

Although water makes up the bulk volume of the finished beer, it is often the least discussed ingredient. However, water interacts with brewing ingredients and can contribute to the aroma and flavor of the finished beer. Primary considerations in evaluating the suitability of a water source for brewing are chlorination, pH, and mineral content.

YEAST CHART

Yeast Type and Examples	General Characteristics
American American, California	Clean-fermenting with low fruitiness; medium flocculator; recommended temperature range of 65°F–72°F; quite versatile and excellent for hoppy ales
British English, British	Clean-fermenting with characteristics that highlight the malt character; highly flocculant; recommended temperature range of 65°F–72°F; works well in malty beers but quite versatile
Irish Irish	Produces a fruity yet crisp beer; excellent for dark beers; medium to high flocculator; recommended fermentation temperatures of 62°F–70°F; excellent for traditional stouts
Belgian Abbey, Trappist, Belgian	Varies but generally produces more esters and phenols than American and British yeasts; typically medium flocculators with a slightly higher temperature tolerance than American and British strains; some Belgian yeasts have a high alcohol tolerance; excellent for Belgian ales such as Dubbels or Trippels
Saison Belgian, French, Belle	Most produce a fruity, spicy, earthy beer, are medium flocculators, and tolerate higher fermentation temperatures; excellent yeast to use in warm weather
Wheat Hefeweizen, Belgian Wit, American	Produces characteristics specific to various wheat ales—banana and clove in German styles, spice and fruit in Belgian styles and clean American styles; generally a low flocculator with ideal fermentation temperatures in the 65°F–70°F range
Lager German, Czech, American, Munich	Used for lager beers with clean profiles, though some strains emphasize the malt or hop character of the beer; flocculation varies; fermentation temperature range 48°F–55°F generally
Brettanomyces *B. lambicus,* *B. bruxellensis*	Wild yeast that may be used as a primary yeast or in secondary; behaves similar to *S. cerevisiae* when used in primary and adds a funky, farmhouse character in secondary

Buying purified spring water for brewing is the easiest route, as it guarantees you'll have a neutral water free of impurities and chlorine. However, municipal water supplies are often just fine for brewing. The most important thing to do when brewing from the tap is to filter your water through charcoal or use Campden tablets to treat it. This is necessary because nearly all municipal waters are chlorinated, whether with chlorine or chloramine. While chlorine dissipates when boiled, chloramine needs to be removed by carbon filtration or the use of Campden tablets ahead of the boil.

Mineral content can vary greatly by region, so do a little research to figure out if your water is soft or hard. Your city may be able to provide you with the data, and many local homebrew stores will have this information as well. Hard water, meaning water with high mineral content, will have more character—this can be a good or bad thing. Some cities with famously hard water, mostly in England, have used it to their advantage in crafting signature styles. Some brewers may add mineral salts to their water if it's soft, particularly when they're trying for a particular style, but we won't use these additions for the recipes in this book. Generally, if your water tastes good, it's probably good enough to brew with as long as it's been properly filtered. If you're using tap water to brew, I recommend installing an under-sink, in-line charcoal filter on the cold water tap in your kitchen. Single-unit under-sink filters are inexpensive, effective, and convenient for all of your brewing needs.

HOW to BREW (the BIAB WAY)

The following equipment and instructions are scaled for a 2-gallon batch size, a comfortable size for the stovetop.

Materials
- Basic brewing equipment (pages 17–24)
- Cleanser and sanitizer
- 4–5 gal. stainless-steel pot
- Brew bag (slightly larger than your brew pot)
- Stainless-steel colander or vegetable steamer that fits inside your pot
- Old towels or blankets to wrap your pot in (if your brew kettle does not fit in your oven)
- Stainless-steel long-handled spoon

- Thermometer
- 2.5-gal. (or larger) fermentation bucket or carboy
- Airlock or blow-off tube (and bung if using a carboy)
- Hydrometer
- Packaging equipment (for kegging or bottling)
- Recipe and ingredients
- 3 gal. filtered water
- Bungee cords
- Brewing notebook

Optional Equipment
- Livestock bucket heater (if your stove has trouble getting the wort to a vigorous boil)
- Mash pH stabilizer
- Perforated pizza pan and springform ring or additional colander
- Wooden dowel or silicone long-handled spoon (to mark as a measuring stick for your pot)
- Wort chiller
- Auto-siphon or racking cane and tubing
- Brewing software or app (see Resources, page 186)

51

Instructions

1. Fill the pot with 2.75 gallons of water. Place a metal colander in the bottom of the pot, insert the probe of a wired kitchen thermometer, and turn the burner on high. The colander will prevent your grain bag from sitting on the bottom of the pot and potentially getting scorched or melted by the heat.

2. Preheat your oven to the lowest setting. You want it to be somewhere in the 150–175°F range.

3. Bring the water in the pot to strike temperature (the temperature at which you add the grain), which can vary based on the amount of grain you're using and the target mash temperature. As the water temperature drops slightly when the grain is added, your strike temperature will be slightly higher than the desired mash temperature. I typically shoot for 162°F for low-gravity beers, which I mash at 154°F.

4. Once the water is at strike temperature, insert the brew bag, securing it around the edge of the pot with a bungee cord. Add the crushed grain slowly, stirring continuously to avoid forming dough

balls. (I also add a pH mash stabilizer here when brewing with all pale malts.) Adding the grain and stirring should bring the mash temperature down to about 154°F.

Note: If the mash is too hot, you can add a few ice cubes (made with filtered water) and stir until you reach the desired temperature. If the mash is too cool, turn on your burner and stir until the mash warms up to the proper temperature.

5. Turn off the oven, place the lid on your pot, and place the pot in the preheated oven. Set your timer for an hour. The mash typically loses only 1 degree per hour using the preheated oven approach, but it's a good idea to check it halfway through the first time, in case your oven runs hot or cold.

6. After an hour has passed, remove the brew kettle and place it back on the burner. Turn the burner on high and bring the temperature to mash-out, about 170°F. Leave the burner on and lift the grain bag out with your left hand while placing the perforated pizza pan with a springform ring on top of the pot with your right hand. Lower the grain bag onto the pizza pan, keeping it enclosed in the

springform ring. Allow the bag to drain for 10 minutes.

7. After the bag has drained for 10 minutes, *gently* squeeze and remove it, along with the pizza pan and springform ring.

8. Stir the wort and remove a sample to take a gravity reading. You'll have to let the sample cool to room temperature in an ice bath before taking the reading; if you want to speed up this process, place the liquid in a cocktail shaker with thin metal walls and agitate it in the ice bath.

53

9. Bring the wort to a boil, then add the 60-minute hop addition and set your timer for 45 minutes. I use the boil time to clean the fermentation vessel and fill it with sanitizing solution. I also mix up a second container of sanitizing solution for my instant-read thermometer, yeast container, scissors, airlock, and plastic strainer. Remember to add hops to the boil at the appropriate time if you have any additions before 15 minutes.

10. Once the timer goes off, add the wort chiller to the brew kettle. Set the timer for 5 minutes. When this timer goes off, add the yeast nutrient, stir the wort, and set the timer for the final 10 minutes. (Again, remember to add hops during the last 15 minutes per the recipe you're following.)

11. Once the timer goes off after the last 10 minutes, turn off the burner and run cold water through the chiller to cool the wort. The most important factor in reducing contamination of your wort is to chill it quickly, in less than 30 minutes. Most brewers choose to sanitize the pot's lid and place it

back on the pot. Agitate the wort periodically to help it cool either by stirring with a sanitized spoon or, if you can lift the pot, by swirling it around. Once it's near room temperature, take a reading with your sanitized thermometer and continue to cool until you reach the pitching temperature for your yeast.

12. Once you reach pitching temperature, turn off the water and remove the wort chiller. Remove enough wort with a sanitized container to take a gravity reading.

13. Empty the fermentation vessel of sanitizing solution and transfer the wort from the pot to the vessel by pouring it through a sanitized plastic strainer or racking with a sanitized racking cane and tubing. If you pour your wort, you will provide enough aeration for the low-gravity beers in this chapter. If you use the tubing, make sure to shake the wort in your fermenter or stir with a sanitized spoon for a couple of minutes to aerate.

14. Pitch the yeast, place the lid or stopper and airlock on the fermentation vessel, and let the magic happen. Remember to monitor the temperature

of your fermentation and keep it in the appropriate range for the yeast.

Note: Fermentation temperature control is especially important in the first few days of the ferment. Yeast create a good amount of heat as they do their job, and off-flavors from fermentation usually occur when brewers either ferment at too-high temperatures or have large fluctuations in temperature during the first few days. Once the yeast have done the bulk of the work, you can safely let the temperature rise to the upper end of the recommended range.

BIA HOI

OG: 1.033 | FG: 1.007 | ABV: 3.4% | IBU: 8–10 | Carbonation: high

Stroll the sidewalks of cities like Hanoi or Hoi An, and you'll stumble upon a cluster of small plastic chairs with a nearby sign reading "Fresh Beer" or "Bia Hoi." Take a seat, and a server will bring you a fresh glass of bia hoi, poured either directly from the keg or a plastic jug. It's low-alcohol and very refreshing, a Pilsner adaptation that is brewed with up to 50 percent rice and allowed to ferment only a couple of days. (It uses a lager yeast but is fermented at ale temperatures.) Bia hoi is designed to be drunk fresh, with a keg lasting for 24 hours or less. This is an easy beer and delightfully thirst-quenching in warm weather. This particular recipe is inspired by the bia hoi brewed by Malai Kitchen in Dallas, Texas. **Yield: *2 gallons***

- **2.75 gal. filtered, chlorine-free water**
- **1 lb. 12 oz. Pilsen malt, crushed**
- **8 oz. rice syrup solids, available from your homebrew supplier**
- **½ oz. Hallertauer hop pellets (4.1% AA)**
- **½ packet German lager yeast (wet or dry)**
- **⅛ tsp. beer yeast nutrient**

Instructions

For complete brewing instructions, see pages 50–55.

1. Heat 2.75 gallons of water to 162°F and mix in the crushed Pilsen malt. The mash temperature should be 154°F. Place in the oven and mash for 60 minutes.

2. After 60 minutes, place the mash back on the stove. Heat to 170°F for mash-out.

3. Remove and drain your grain bag into the kettle.

4. Bring the wort to a boil. Once the boil is rolling, stir in the rice syrup solids. You may want to turn off the heat during this addition to avoid scorching on the bottom of the pot.

5. Bring the wort back to a boil, add the hops, and boil for 45 minutes. Then, with 15 minutes left in the boil, add your chiller. With 10 minutes left, add the yeast nutrient.

6. After 60 minutes of boil time, turn off the heat, start running water through the chiller, and chill the wort to the pitching temperature for your yeast.

7. Transfer to a sanitized fermentation vessel, reserving some of the wort for a gravity reading. Pitch the yeast.

8. Ferment at 67°F to 68°F. The fermentation should finish in 4 to 5 days. Once you see the signs that fermentation is finished, wait another 5 days and then proceed to packaging (see pages 26 to 31).

57

PENNSYLVANIA SWANKEY

OG: 1.032 | FG: 1.008 | ABV: 3.1% | IBU: 8-10 | Carbonation: medium

Historically, Pennsylvania Swankey was a very low-alcohol brown ale brewed with a "flavoring condiment" such as anise seed. Fermentation was stopped early, resulting in a 1 percent ABV beer that could be considered a "temperance beverage." Swankeys were all but extinct by the turn of the twentieth century. The style has lived on at a slightly higher ABV in the homebrewing community and has been resurrected recently by a couple of commercial breweries. It's a fast-fermented mild ale that can be brewed with a variety of spices. I like to use star anise and anise seed, but there are a few variations recommended at the end of this recipe as well. This is a fun beer with a fun name—who can resist a pint of Swankey? **Yield: *2 gallons***

- **2.75 gal. filtered, chlorine-free water**
- **2 lb. 4 oz. two-row pale base malt, crushed**
- **1.5 oz. chocolate malt, crushed**
- **3 oz. brown sugar such as panela**
- **0.15 oz. Goldings hop pellets (5.8% AA)**
- **1 star anise pod**
- **¼ tsp. plus ⅛ tsp. anise seed**
- **½ packet English ale yeast (wet or dry)**
- **⅛ tsp. beer yeast nutrient**

Instructions

For complete brewing instructions, see pages 50–55.

1. Heat 2.75 gallons of water to 164°F and mix in the crushed malt. The mash temperature should be 156°F. Place in the oven and mash for 60 minutes.

2. After 60 minutes, place the mash back on the stove. Heat to 170°F for mash-out.

3. Remove and drain your grain bag into the kettle.

4. Bring the wort to a boil. Once the boil is rolling, stir in the sugar. You may want to turn off the heat to avoid scorching on the bottom of the pot.

5. Bring the wort back to a boil, add the hops, and boil for 45 minutes. Then, with 15 minutes left in the boil, add your chiller. With 10 minutes left,

add the yeast nutrient. With 5 minutes left, add the star anise and anise seed.

6. After 60 minutes of boil time, turn off the heat and start running water through the chiller and chill the wort to the pitching temperature for your yeast.

7. Transfer to a sanitized fermentation vessel, reserving some of the wort for a gravity reading. Pitch the yeast.

8. Ferment at 67°F to 68°F. The fermentation should finish in 4 to 5 days. Once you see the signs that fermentation is finished, wait another 5 days and then proceed to bottling (see pages 26 to 31).

Variations

- **Chai Swankey**: Omit the anise seed and star anise. Add 1–2 chai tea bags at flame-out. I prefer the Rooibos-based versions over the black tea versions, but this is personal preference.
- **Rosemary Swankey:** Omit the anise seed and star anise and add a couple of sprigs of fresh rosemary at 5 minutes instead. An Abbey ale yeast will add a complementary character to the rosemary.
- **Spruce Swankey:** Spruce was a traditional Colonial American beer flavoring and works well with this historic style. Omit the anise seed and star anise and use a tablespoon or so of spruce tips at 5 minutes.

BRISK BEER

SMOKED SUMMER ALE

OG: 1.040 | FG: 1.009 | ABV: 4.1% | IBU: 8-10 | Carbonation: medium

I absolutely adore smoked beers. They can range from just a hint of smoke to something that may be described as bacon in a glass. This recipe produces a blonde ale balanced with a subdued smokiness, a sessionable ale that appeals to almost everyone. It uses wheat for added depth and body. I love the beechwood-smoked malt, but other smoked malts may be used; variations follow the recipe. **Yield: *2 gallons***

- **2.75 gal. filtered, chlorine-free water**
- **1 lb. 10 oz. two-row pale base malt, crushed**
- **10 oz. beechwood-smoked malt, crushed**
- **10 oz. wheat malt, crushed**
- **0.3 oz. Crystal hop pellets (4.3% AA)**
- **²/₃ packet English ale yeast (wet or dry)**
- **¹/₈ tsp. beer yeast nutrient**

Instructions

For complete brewing instructions, see pages 50–55.

1. Heat 2.75 gallons of water to 162°F and mix in the crushed malt. The mash temperature should be 154°F. Place in the oven and mash for 60 minutes.
2. After 60 minutes, place the mash back on the stove. Heat to 170°F for mash-out.
3. Remove and drain your grain bag into the kettle.
4. Bring the wort to a boil. Once the boil is rolling, add the hops and boil for 45 minutes. Then, with 15 minutes left in the boil, add your chiller. With 10 minutes left, add the yeast nutrient.
5. After 60 minutes of boil time, turn off the heat, start running water through the chiller, and chill the wort to the pitching temperature for your yeast.
6. Transfer to a sanitized fermentation vessel, reserving some of the wort for a gravity reading. Pitch the yeast.
7. Ferment at 67°F to 68°F. The fermentation should finish in 4 to 5 days. Once you see the signs that fermentation is finished, wait another 5 days and then proceed to bottling (see pages 26 to 31).

Variations

- **Oak-Smoked (or Cherrywood-Smoked) Summer Ale:** Use 2 pounds 4 ounces of pale malt and 10 ounces of oak-smoked wheat malt in place of the malt bill. For cherrywood, use the recipes as is, substituting cherrywood-smoked malt for the beechwood-smoked malt.

- **Home-Smoked Ale:** If you have a smoker and a backyard, it's easy to smoke your malt with the wood chips of your choice. Start by soaking your wood chips overnight. Use aluminum screening to hold your malt in the top of your smoker. Smoke the malt for 10 to 30 minutes, using a spray bottle of filtered water to keep the malt damp and stirring frequently. Spread the malt on a baking sheet or similar surface to dry fully, then place in a sealed container. Condition for 1 to 2 weeks, and your home-smoked malt will be ready to use. The amount of smoke character can vary, so it's best to start with a conservative amount, such as the 10 ounces in this recipe, but you may wish to go higher or lower.

GALENA SMASH SESSION IPA

OG: 1.041 | FG: 1.009 | ABV: 4.1% | IBU: 28–30 | Carbonation: medium

Single malt and single hop (SMASH) is a simple type of beer that highlights the beauty of just one hop and one malt. SMASH beers not only are a great way to learn the ins and outs of a hop variety but also employ a technique called hop bursting, adding all of your hops late in the boil. Hop bursting gives you big aroma and flavor while still adding bittering balance to your beer. I've chosen Galena for the hop in this recipe, as it contributes a lovely citrusy, fruity spiciness to the aroma and flavor, with a juicy fruit quality. It is also widely available and inexpensive. Feel free to swap out the Galena with your favorite hop or one that you would like more experience with; use brewing software or an app to adjust the hop quantities if the hop you choose has a different AA percentage. This is a sessionable pale ale with a burst of hop aroma and flavor. **Yield: *2 gallons***

- 2.75 gal. filtered, chlorine-free water
- 3 lb. two-row pale base malt, crushed
- 1.8 oz. Galena hop pellets (11.4% AA)
- 0.4 oz Galena hop pellets added 10 minutes before end of boil
- 0.5 oz Galena hop pellets added 5 minutes before end of boil
- 0.5 oz Galena hop pellets added at flame-out
- 0.4 oz Galena hop pellets added at dry hopping (optional)
- ⅔ packet American ale yeast (wet or dry)
- ⅛ tsp. beer yeast nutrient

Instructions
For complete brewing instructions, see pages 50–55.

1. Heat 2.75 gallons of water to 162°F and mix in the crushed pale base malt. The mash temperature should be 154°F. Place in the oven and mash for 60 minutes.

2. After 60 minutes, place the mash back on the stove. Heat to 170°F for mash-out.

3. Remove and drain your grain bag into the kettle.

4. Bring the wort to a boil. With 15 minutes left in the boil, add your chiller. With 10 minutes

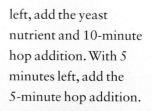

left, add the yeast nutrient and 10-minute hop addition. With 5 minutes left, add the 5-minute hop addition.

5. After 60 minutes of boil time, add your flame-out hop addition, turn off the heat and start running water through the chiller, and chill the wort to the pitching temperature for your yeast.

6. Transfer to a sanitized fermentation vessel, reserving some of the wort for a gravity reading. Pitch the yeast.

7. Ferment at 67°F to 68°F. The fermentation should finish in 4 to 5 days. Once you see the signs that fermentation is finished, wait another 5 days and then proceed to bottling (see pages 26 to 31). If you wish to dry hop, add 0.4 oz. Galena hops 3 days before you bottle.

GOSE WITH SMOKED SALT AND LEMONGRASS

OG: 1.051 | FG: 1.011 | ABV: 5.2% | IBU: 10–12 | Carbonation: high

Gose is a tart, salty, slightly herbal low-alcohol ale that originates in Goslar, Germany. This might sound like a strange combination if you've never had one, but it is a beautiful, thirst-quenching beer that packs in a lot of flavor. Traditionally, it was spontaneously fermented with ambient yeast, but brewers began using a combination of ale yeast and *Lactobacillus* instead sometime in the late 1800s. This version uses acidulated malt, a light-colored specialty malt that has been sprayed with lactic acid, instead of *Lactobacillus* bacteria. *Lacto-bacillus* can be a tricky organism to brew with and requires a longer fermentation time than brewer's yeast. Acidulated malt generally adds a softer, milder tartness than *Lactobacillus*, making this an ideal opportunity to add depth in other ways. Traditional goses are brewed with salt and coriander, but this recipe uses smoked salt and lemongrass and is fermented with an English ale yeast to add further dimension. This makes for a fruity, lightly tart, salty, lemony beer with the barest wisp of smoke. **Yield: *2 gallons***

- **2.75 gal. filtered, chlorine-free water**
- **1 lb. 8 oz. two-row wheat base malt, crushed**
- **1 lb. 4 oz. Pilsner base malt, crushed**
- **12 oz. acidulated malt, crushed separately from the wheat and Pilsner malts**
- **0.3 oz. Hallertauer hop pellets (4.1% AA)**
- **0.5 oz. lemongrass, diced**
- **0.25 oz. smoked salt, found at specialty food stores**
- **¾ packet English ale yeast (wet or dry)**
- **⅛ tsp. beer yeast nutrient**

Note: As acidulated malt can lower the pH of the mash, this recipe requires a two-part mash. The wheat and Pilsner malts will be mashed together for 45 minutes, then the acidulated malt will be added and an additional mash conducted for 30 minutes. Therefore, you'll want to keep your acidulated malt separate from your wheat and Pilsner malts.

Instructions

For complete brewing instructions, see pages 50–55.

1. Heat 2.75 gallons of water to 157°F and mix in the crushed wheat and Pilsner base malts. The mash temperature should be 151°F. Place in the oven and mash for 45 minutes.

2. After 45 minutes, add the crushed acidulated malt and mash for an additional 30 minutes.

3. After 30 more minutes, place the mash back on the stove. Heat to 170°F for mash-out.

4. Remove and drain your grain bag into the kettle.

5. Bring the wort to a boil. Once the boil is rolling, add the hops and boil for 45 minutes. With 15 minutes left in the boil, add your chiller. With 10 minutes left, add the yeast nutrient. With 5 minutes left, add the lemongrass and smoked salt.

6. After 60 minutes of boil time, turn off the heat, start running water through the chiller, and chill the wort to the pitching temperature for your yeast.

7. Transfer to a sanitized fermentation vessel, straining out the lemongrass and reserving some of the wort for a gravity reading. Pitch the yeast.

8. Ferment at 67°F to 68°F. The fermentation should finish in 4 to 5 days. Once you see the signs that fermentation is finished, wait another 5 days and then proceed to bottling (see page 26 to 31).

Variations

- **Unsmoked Gose:** Go traditional and use regular sea salt instead of the smoked version and 0.2 ounces crushed coriander seed in place of the lemongrass.

- **Puckered Gose:** For a more pronounced tartness, use the kettle-souring method described in the Berliner Weisse recipe on page 68.

- **Old Bay Gose:** I've had a couple of goses that used Old Bay seasoning in place of the salt—I was leery at first, but they were both delicious. There are also a myriad of flavored salts available in gourmet markets; pick one and choose an herb or spice that jives with it. I bet a mango-chili salt gose would be lovely.

BERLINER WEISSE

OG: 1.041 | FG: 1.009 | ABV: 4.1% | IBU: 8-10 | Carbonation: high

Berliner Weisse is another slightly tart, low-alcohol thirst quencher. This version incorporates a technique called kettle souring. We'll mash as usual, add uncrushed grain to the wort, and allow the natural *Lactobacillus* on the grain to sour the wort in a controlled temperature setting. The wort is then boiled and fermented as normal. Kettle souring minimizes the risk of contamination to your brewing system and is also more predictable than sour mashing or primary fermentation with *Lactobacillus*. This technique may be used to produce other *Lacto*-driven beers by changing up the malt bill, using a different yeast, or adding flavorings. **Yield: *2 gallons***

Kettle Souring Equipment
- Chest cooler large enough to fit your brew kettle inside (with the lid closed)
- Aquarium heaters (help prevent heat loss inside the cooler but are not strictly necessary)
- Duct tape

- **2.75 gal. filtered, chlorine-free water**
- **1 lb. 8 oz. Pilsen base malt, crushed**
- **1 lb. 8 oz. wheat base malt, crushed**
- **0.5 oz. Hersbrucker hop pellets (2.5% AA)**
- **2/3 packet English ale yeast (wet or dry)**
- **1/8 tsp. beer yeast nutrient**

Instructions
For complete brewing instructions, see pages 50–55.

1. Heat 2.75 gallons of water to 156°F and mix in the crushed malt. The mash temperature should be 151°F. Place in the oven and mash for 60 minutes.
2. After 60 minutes, place the mash back on the stove. Heat to 170°F for mash-out.
3. Remove and drain your grain bag into the kettle.
4. Chill the wort to 120°F in an ice bath. On a separate burner, bring 2 gallons of water to a boil. Preheat the cooler by filling with hot tap water and emptying. If using aquarium heaters, place these inside the cooler.

5. Add ½ cup of uncrushed base malt to the brew kettle. Flush with carbon dioxide (optional if you don't have a kegging setup), place the probe of your wired thermometer inside the kettle, place the lid on the kettle, and seal with duct tape.

6. Place the kettle inside the cooler and add enough hot tap water to reach the level of the liquid inside your kettle (supplementing with the off-boil water that you heated in step 4). The amount and temperature of the water will vary depending on the size of your cooler.

7. Close the lid of the cooler and plug in the probe of your thermometer and your aquarium heaters, if using. The temperature of your mash should be between 115°F and 118°F.

8. Kettle sour for 24 to 60 hours, depending on the desired sourness. Over this time, remove cooled water and add hot tap water or off-boil water as needed to maintain temperatures between 115°F and 118°F. I remove water three times a day—in the morning, after work, and before I go to sleep. I generally kettle-sour for 48 hours, which brings the pH of the mash down to 3.6 to 3.8.

9. After the kettle sour has completed, remove your kettle and return to the stovetop. Remove most of the souring grain by dipping a meshed strainer into the wort.

10. Bring the wort to a boil. Once the boil is rolling, add the hops and boil for 45 minutes. Then, with 15 minutes left in the boil, add your chiller. With 10 minutes left, add the yeast nutrient.

11. After 60 minutes of boil time, turn off the heat, start running water through the chiller, and chill the wort to the pitching temperature for your yeast.

12. Transfer to a sanitized fermentation vessel, reserving some of the wort for a gravity reading. Pitch the yeast.

13. Ferment at 67°F to 68°F. The fermentation should finish in 4 to 5 days. Once you see the signs that fermentation is finished, wait another 5 days and then proceed to bottling (see page 26 to 31).

FAUX FLANDERS RED ALE

OG: 1.057 | FG: 1.013 | ABV: 5.8% | IBU: 15 | Carbonation: high

The Flanders red ale is a wonderfully complex sour from northern Belgium. It is made with a variety of malts; fermented with an assortment of yeasts and bacteria, including *Lactobacillus*, *Pediococcus*, *Brettanomyces*, and *Acetobacter*; and aged in oak barrels. Flanders red ales traditionally take two years or more to finish and are often blended before being bottled. While I've brewed traditional Flanders red ales at home, doing so is a commitment and requires a lot of patience. I used my experience in brewing and aging more complex sours to create this simple rendition. It is by no means a true Flanders red, but by blending a basic Flanders red base beer with a complex boozy kombucha, you can create a delicious sessionable ale with complex notes. **Yield: *2 gallons***

Flanders ale base

- **2.75 gal. filtered, chlorine-free water**
- **1 lb. 5 oz. Pilsen base malt, crushed**
- **1 lb. 5 oz. Munich base malt, crushed**
- **1 lb. 5 oz. Vienna base malt, crushed**
- **3 oz. CaraMunich malt, crushed**
- **3 oz. Crystal 120 or Special B malt, crushed**
- **3 oz. wheat malt, crushed**
- **0.3 oz. Kent Goldings hop pellets (5.8% AA)**
- **1 packet English or Belgian ale yeast, Abbey or Trappist (wet or dry)**
- **⅛ tsp. beer yeast nutrient**

Boozy kombucha base

- **½ gal. fermented kombucha**
- **½ c. frozen tart cherries, thawed and macerated, or ¼ c. 100% tart cherry juice**
- **1 tbsp. preboiled light roast oak chips, boiled for 15 minutes, drained and dried**
- **¼ c. sugar**
- **¼ c. champagne yeast**

Note: When I make this beer, I split the 2-gallon batch into 2 1-gallon jugs and ferment half with English ale yeast and half with Belgian ale yeast. This gives me more flexibility in blending and a more complex beer overall. If you're choosing only one yeast, the Belgian ale yeast will give you a beer with more esters and phenols.

Instructions

For complete brewing instructions, see pages 50–55.

1. Heat 2.75 gallons of water to 162°F and mix in the crushed malt. The mash temperature should be 154°F. Place in the oven and mash for 60 minutes.

2. After 60 minutes, place the mash back on the stove. Heat to 170°F for mash-out.

3. Remove and drain your grain bag into the kettle.

4. Bring the wort to a boil. Once the boil is rolling, add the hops, and boil for 45 minutes. Then, with 15 minutes left in the boil, add your chiller. With 10 minutes left, add the yeast nutrient.

5. After 60 minutes of boil time, turn off the heat, start running water through the chiller, and chill the wort to the pitching temperature for your yeast.

6. Transfer to a sanitized fermentation vessel, reserving some of the wort for a gravity reading. Pitch the yeast. Ferment at 67°F to 68°F. The fermentation should finish in 5 to 7 days.

7. On the same day that you brew the Flanders ale base, brew a boozy kombucha following the directions on page 127, using the preboiled wood chips and cherries or cherry juice for flavorings. Pitch the yeast and ferment for 5 to 7 days.

8. After 3 to 5 additional days, blend the Flanders base beer and the boozy kombucha to your taste and package according to directions on pages 26 to 31. To determine the blending ratio, I pull samples from all of my base beverages and blend using 1-tablespoon amounts until I determine the desired blending ratio. For instance, I might do three different sample blends for this beer, the first with 1 tablespoon ale base and 1 tablespoon boozy buch base, the second with 3 tablespoons ale base and 1 tablespoon boozy buch base, and the last with 3 tablespoons boozy buch base and 1 tablespoon ale base. I then use my favorite ratio to blend the beverages.

DEVELOPING YOUR OWN BRISK BEER

ALWAYS BEGIN designing a new recipe by imagining the beer in my head. I picture the glass and take an imaginary sniff, then a sip. I think about where the imagined aromas, flavors, mouthfeel, and color come from and which malts, yeast, hops, and flavorings might create them. I think about what styles are similar and then take a look at my own recipes as well as those I find on the Internet or in my favorite homebrewing books. If I'm adapting another recipe, I plug the recipe into my brewing app to get the malt percentages, IBU, and gravities. If I'm adapting a higher-gravity beer recipe to a lower-gravity beer, I use the malt percentages to build my recipe instead of the weights of the grain. I do the same when I'm moving from a larger batch to a smaller batch or vice versa. If I'm using a flavoring, such as a spice or herb, that I've never used before, I take a look at other recipes that have used it and survey the amounts used along with where and when they've used it. When designing lower-alcohol session beers, I think about where I'll get the most bang for my buck as far as aroma or flavor—it could be by souring or by using herbs or spices, distinct malts, or a highly flavorful yeast.

Homebrewing has become wildly popular in the last decade or two. Commercial beer is also thriving, with more styles of beer available now than ever. Traditional styles are being riffed on, extinct styles have been revived, and new styles are being invented. Brewers are throwing just about every imaginable ingredient into their beer. As a result, a wider variety of raw ingredients are available to brewers, and more local producers are appearing on the scene.

Browse a local homebrew supply store or online homebrew vendor, and you will be amazed at the varieties of hops, malts, and yeasts available to you as a homebrewer. It's almost overwhelming, but it also means that you can create almost any beer that you can dream up, be it a beloved commercial beer, an archaic beverage you've stumbled upon in a text, or the beer you think would pair with your favorite food. The homebrewing world is your oyster!

3

SHORT MEAD

M Y FIRST ENCOUNTER with mead was at the New York City Home-brewers Guild annual mead meeting in May 2006. This is always one of the biggest meetings of the year; people travel hundreds of miles to attend and share their homemade meads. They even bring their own special mead goblets and wear horned Viking helmets. There are many more varieties of mead poured than you can possibly sample in one evening. The speaker was a local beekeeper and mead maker from Long Island who brought a drawer of live bees along with bottles of his mead. We were crammed into a tiny bar in the East Village neighborhood of Manhattan, and those bees were propped up on a wobbly table that was bumped more and more as the night went on. Thankfully no bees escaped, but that was a memorable night for many reasons—most importantly, because I fell in love with mead.

Many of you are probably familiar with mead as well. But what about short mead? When I say "short mead," I'm not referring to the size of the pour! A short mead is simply a lower-alcohol mead. You might think of them as session meads, as they are usually around 5 percent alcohol and very drinkable. They also take less than two weeks to go from the proverbial honey pot to glass and are a fantastic canvas for a wide variety of flavorings.

FROM MEAD to SHORT MEAD

RESEARCHERS HAVE FOUND evidence of a fermented beverage made from rice, honey, and fruit dating back to 7000 to 6600 BCE, making mead the earliest recorded alcoholic beverage in human history. Mead continued to be a very popular beverage through ancient Greek times, was mentioned in the classic epic poem *Beowulf*, and is currently enjoyed in many parts of the world. It's still a rather obscure beverage in modern America, but that's beginning to change.

A good mead is like liquid gold, a balance of sweetness and alcohol in a full-bodied yet silky-smooth beverage. Alas, that alcohol sneaks up on you quickly; most meads are between 12 and 15 percent ABV, similar to wines. Meads also require patience, taking anywhere from one month to a year or more to create, depending on the technique and style.

That's the main reason that while I love to taste meads, I had no interest in making them until a friend of mine introduced me to a little beverage she called short mead, which she made from a kit (picked up at a sheep and wool festival, of all places). I still remember my first taste of that elderflower short mead—wowza! It was a clean, carbonated, refreshing, yet flavorful drink.

It was quite different from the traditional meads I knew but every bit as delicious. Better yet, it only took a week or two to make, since it was a mere 5 percent ABV. I was in love all over again. I ordered my own kits and got to work. Many years and batches later, short mead is one of my favorite beverages to brew. It's one of the easiest libations to make at home and is a wonderful way to explore flavors and express your creativity. And unlike polarizing bitter beers or strong honey wine, almost everyone loves short meads. I hope you find them just as delightful as I do.

Styles

There are many different styles of mead. Here are a few of the recognized variations.

Acerglyn. Acerglyn is a mead made with honey and maple syrup. After friends taste this one, they commonly remark, "I want pancakes with this." Acerglyn is a dry, refreshing mead with notes of maple in the nose and on the tongue. I like to use Grade B maple syrup for a richer aroma and flavor. If you live in a maple-growing area, you could even substitute maple sap for the water when making your short mead for an interesting variation.

Bochet. Bochet is a mead made with caramelized or "burned" honey. Caramelizing a portion of the honey adds richness to the aroma and flavor of the mead. Think of tasting a simple syrup made with white sugar alongside one made with brown sugar; both are sweet, but the brown sugar has a different depth. Bochets are lovely on their own but provide a nice foil for other flavoring additions as well. I find that using caramelized honey in a short mead adds more of a honey backbone without adding an intense caramel aroma and flavor.

Braggot. Braggot is a mead-beer hybrid. Braggots are commonly created by brewing a beer with malt and honey, though they can also be created by brewing a beer and a mead separately and blending

them together. Braggots can run the gamut from saisons to sours to rich barley wine combinations, depending on your malt and yeast choices. This is a style that begs for creativity.

Capsicumel. Capsicumel is a mead made with honey and chili peppers. A touch of chili heat is the perfect complement to the light sweetness of short mead. Keep in mind that chili peppers not only come in a wide range of heat levels, measured in Scoville units, but also vary in aroma and flavor. You can control the level of heat easily by the amount of peppers you add. Chili peppers can be used fresh or dried and can be roasted or smoked for more flavor options.

Cyser. Cyser is a cider-mead hybrid. Cysers are typically made by fermenting honey and apple juice, using the juice in place of part or all of the water.

Melomel. Melomel is a mead made with honey and fruit. Your short mead will reflect the aroma and flavor characteristics of the fruit that you're adding. I've tasted all kinds of fruit meads, from raspberry to cantaloupe to durian and everything in between. Mead can be a perfect beverage to showcase locally-grown seasonal fruit or that exotic fruit that you pick up at your local international market.

Metheglin. Metheglin is a mead made with herbs and/or spices. Meads are wonderful backgrounds for a wide variety of herbs and spices. Single-herb or single-spice meads such as rosemary mead and black pepper mead are lovely, as are "kitchen sink" spiced meads. Your limits are dictated merely by the depth of your spice cabinet.

Pyment. Pyment is a beverage made with honey and grapes and/or grape juice. Pyments combine the beauty of traditional wine and honey in one glass. The flavor depends largely on the type of grape or grape juice you use. Pyments may be made with store-bought grape juice or hand-crushed wine grapes.

Sima. Sima is a Finnish beverage traditionally made with honey and lemons. Sima is a refreshing, lightly tart beverage perfect for the summer months.

Tej. Tej is an Ethiopian mead made with honey and gesho, a plant native to Ethiopia. The gesho adds a slight bitterness, balancing the sweetness of the honey. Although gesho may be difficult to find, you could make a variation by brewing a tea made from bark or hops to add to your short mead.

Viking blood. Viking blood is a mead made with honey and cherry juice. This is a deep red variation of mead and is one of my favorite beverages to bring to Halloween parties.

INGREDIENTS

Honey

There are many varieties and qualities of honey available, but honey is usually classified by the floral source of the nectar that the bees used. Wildflower honey is common and is derived from many different types of flowers. You can also find single varietal honeys such as clover, orange blossom, buckwheat, chestnut, and so on. Some apiaries also designate their honey by the seasons: spring, summer, and fall. The aroma and flavor of these honeys can differ considerably.

You can use almost any of these honeys for your mead. In short meads, a lot of the aroma and flavors of the honey may be fermented out or masked by other additives such as fruit or spices anyway. If you are making a flavored mead, a mild-flavored honey is absolutely acceptable. My favorite honey to use regardless of the type of mead I'm making is local honey. I'm fortunate to have several local apiaries sell their honey at my preferred Green Market here in New York City. These honeys cost a bit more than mass-market honey, but I can often buy in bulk for significantly less. I've also found wonderful honey in specialty food stores, and warehouse chains occasionally sell quality honey for an extremely low price. I would avoid imported or low-grade mass-market honeys, though, as recent tests have shown that these may contain contaminants.

Water

Filtered or dechlorinated spring water is essential. Do not use water with chlorine, chloramine, or other hard minerals added.

Yeast

Almost any yeast can be used to brew short mead, but I've found that dry champagne yeast will produce a mead with neutral yeast character in the quickest amount of time. It is not necessary to rehydrate the yeast, but if you do, I recommend using Go-Ferm. (See page 12.) Many varieties of ale yeast will also produce nice short meads but usually take longer to ferment out. I have had good success using American, English, saison, and Abbey-style Belgian ale yeasts. Saison and Belgian yeasts tend to add a herbal or floral nature to the resulting short mead, while American and English ale yeasts leave more of a residual honey character, often with beeswax notes to the beverage.

Yeast Nutrient

You do not need to be as particular about nutrients with short mead as you would be if you were brewing a full-strength mead. I've used everything from beer nutrients to diammonium phosphate (DAP) to Fermaid K with success. I've even forgotten to add nutrients to my short meads, and they have come out just fine. I recommend beer yeast nutrient for the recipes in this book. One-sixteenth of a teaspoon works well for one-gallon batches of short mead. If you don't have a one-sixteenth teaspoon measure (which actually exist), just use around one-fourth of a quarter teaspoon or half of an eighth teaspoon. A pinch will do in a pinch!

Flavorings

There are a myriad of flavorings that may be used in short meads. This is a beverage that begs for creativity! I find inspiration for flavor combinations in recipes, dessert menus, tea stores, books, natural sodas, and cocktail menus. The latter is my favorite source of inspiration. You often don't even need to visit the actual bar or restaurant, as many places post their cocktail menus online.

Fruits. You can use fresh, dried, frozen, or canned fruit or even fruit juices in your meads. Freeze-dried fruits are my favorite, since they are concentrated. They can be more expensive ounce for ounce but are worth the cost, as you can extract more aroma and flavor from a freeze-dried version of a fruit than from any other type. Freeze-dried fruits used to be difficult to track down, but today you can find them at health food stores and groceries that stock gourmet and specialty foods. I recommend rehydrating dried and freeze-dried fruits with off-boil water and steeping just until fully rehydrated. I also pour off-boil water over fresh, frozen, and canned fruits and then cool quickly, either by adding chilled water or placing the container in an ice bath. You may add fresh and frozen fruits directly to your fermenter, but I recommend rinsing them with water first.

Herbs and Spices. You can use fresh or dried herbs and spices. Fresh herbs and spices may lend a different quality of flavor, but you will need to use a larger quantity of fresh compared to dried, and this can take up more room in your fermentation vessel. Keep in mind that dried herbs and spices lose aroma and flavor as they age. Adjust quantity as needed depending on your personal taste and the freshness of the herb or spice. If using dried herbs or spices, steep them in off-boil water for five to fifteen minutes, depending on the freshness of the herb or spice and the flavor desired. I recommend washing fresh herbs or rinsing or dunking them in off-boil water before adding them to your fermentation vessel.

Chili peppers. You can use fresh, dried, or powdered chili peppers.

Teas. Herbal teas are fantastic for flavoring short meads. Although I enjoy creating my own flavor combinations, there are many inventive herbal tea blends available that make delicious meads. These are usually less expensive than buying all of the herbs and spices separately, and they simplify the blending process for you.

Rooibos is a caffeine-free tea made from the leaves of the South African Rooibos bush, also known as red bush. Rooibos is high in antioxidants and is often described as having notes of honey, spice, herbs, flowers, caramel, and wood. It complements short meads beautifully and makes a nice base for a variety of other flavorings. You can also use nonherbal teas in your meads. Lapsang souchong, a smoked black tea, makes a sultry, smoky short mead. See the tea chart on pages 124 and 125 for tea descriptions and ideal steeping temperatures.

HOW to MAKE MEAD

Materials

- 1-gallon jug or wide-mouthed jar
- Sanitizer
- Scale
- Hydrometer
- Recipe and ingredients
- Brewing notebook

Instructions

Short meads are one of the easiest fermented beverages to make. In a nutshell, you're mixing a pound to a pound and a half of honey and any flavorings, if desired, in a gallon of water, adding yeast and nutrients, and letting fermentation happen. Here is the basic process for a one-gallon batch of short mead:

1. Clean and sanitize all equipment, including the 1-gallon jug or wide-mouth jar that will be used as the fermentation vessel. Your honey will be easier to pour and mix in if you

place the honey container in a warm water bath for at least 30 minutes before using.

2. Place the sanitized jug or jar on a kitchen scale and zero it out.

3. Add honey and nutrients to the 1-gallon jug or wide-mouth jar. You may use anywhere from ¾ to 1½ pounds of honey for short meads, depending on your desired ABV. See the honey gravity chart at lower left.

4. Cap or seal and shake to thoroughly combine.

5. Take a gravity reading using a hydrometer, if desired. Your original gravity will be between 1.027 and 1.054, depending on how much honey you used.

6. Pitch yeast and ferment at 66°F to 76°F for 5 to 14 days.

7. When the short mead is at the desired gravity or sweetness, package according to the instructions on pages 26 to 31.

HONEY GRAVITY CHART

for a One-Gallon Batch of Short Mead

The sugar content of honey can vary, depending on type and moisture content. I've used an average to calculate the values in this chart.

Weight of Honey	OG	ABV: FG of 1.008	ABV: FG of 1.004
¾ lb. (12 oz.)	1.027	2.5%	3%
1 lb. (16 oz.)	1.036	3.7%	4.2%
1.25 lb. (20 oz.)	1.045	4.9%	5.4%
1.375 lb. (22 oz.)	1.050	5.6%	6.1%
1.5 lb. (24 oz.)	1.054	6.1%	6.6%

STRAWBERRY-PEPPERCORN SHORT MEAD

Pictured on page 74.

This recipe was one of the first short meads I brewed. I served it at an outdoors art and music benefit bash in Brooklyn, where it was about 100°F outdoors. The strawberry-peppercorn short mead was a huge hit, and the keg kicked in an hour, beating out a slew of beer and cocktails. The spiciness of the peppercorns is a wonderful complement to the sweetness and delicate floral nature of the strawberry. Carbonated lower-alcohol beverages are delightfully refreshing on a hot summer day, but the strawberry aroma will bring you back to warmer times on even the coldest of winter days. **Yield: *1 gallon***

- **1 package (1–1.2 oz.) freeze-dried strawberries**
- **½ tbsp. mixed peppercorns**
- **1.25 lb. honey**
- **1 gal. spring water**
- **¹⁄₁₆ tsp. yeast nutrient**
- **¼ package dry champagne yeast**

Instructions:

1. Place your yeast packet, stopper or lid, airlock, and scissors (to open the yeast packet) into a sanitizing solution. Clean and sanitize a glass jug or jar.

2. Pulverize the freeze-dried strawberries. A small food processor works best, but I've used a mortar and pestle, too. You can also transfer the berries to a zippered plastic bag, squeeze the air out, seal, and hand-crush or use a rolling pin on the berries. Crack the pepper slightly—a mortar and pestle works best for this. Place the crushed berries and peppercorns into a heatproof glass measuring pitcher.

3. Heat 2 cups of water to a boil. A teapot is perfect for this purpose. Pour the off-boil water over your berries and peppercorns, add yeast nutrient, stir, and steep for 10 minutes. After 10 minutes, place your tea in an ice bath to cool to below 75°F.

4. Place the sanitized jug or jar on the scale. Zero the scale and add 1.25 pounds of honey.

5. Remove the jug from the scale, add filtered water leaving enough room for the tea, cap or cover the opening securely, and shake until the honey is combined. Take a look at the bottom of your jug; if honey is still clinging on, keep shaking.

6. Uncap the jug and add the cooled strawberry-peppercorn tea. Do not strain the tea.

7. Top off with water to bring up to 1 gallon, recap or cover, and shake gently to combine. You may take a gravity reading using your hydrometer or refractometer at this point if you like. Your OG will be in the 1.042 to 1.046 range.

8. Uncap, pitch the yeast, and place a stopper or grommeted lid and airlock on the jug.

9. Ferment between 66°F and 76°F for 5 to 14 days.

10. Taste after a week. If it's at your desired sweetness, package using the directions on pages 26 to 31. If it's too sweet, continue to taste every day or every other day until the mead is where you want. Higher fermentation temperatures will increase speed of fermentation. If you are taking gravity readings, I usually find 1.004 to 1.008 to be the ideal range. If you're using fruit or other flavorings that float, I recommend cold-crashing your short mead overnight before bottling. The flavorings will fall to the bottom, and the short mead will be easier to bottle. If you don't cold-crash, I recommend using a filter or strainer to bottle.

Variations

- **Blueberry-Nutmeg Short Mead:** Use a 1- to 1.2-ounce package of freeze-dried blueberries and a dash of freshly grated nutmeg in place of the strawberries and peppercorns. Pulverize your blueberries and follow the directions above.

- **Spiced Cranberry Short Mead:** Use a 1- to 1.2-ounce bag of freeze-dried cranberries and ½ cinnamon stick, 3 cloves, 2 star anise, and a strip of orange zest in place of the strawberries and peppercorns. You do not need to crush the spices; just use them whole. This is a wonderful beverage to serve in late fall and during the winter holidays. It is especially nice with Thanksgiving dinner and may be served warm as well, like a mulled wine.

- **Mango Chili Short Mead:** Use a 1-ounce package of freeze-dried mango and 3 dried pequin chili peppers in place of the strawberries and peppercorns for a spicy, fruity mead. Crush the mango and chilies and use more or less chilies depending on your heat preference.

- **Peach Thyme Short Mead:** Use a 1-ounce package of freeze-dried peaches and ½ teaspoon fresh chopped thyme or a heaping ⅛ teaspoon dried thyme in place of the strawberries and peppercorns.

HERBAL TEA MEAD

When I'm feeling a bit lazy, hurried, or uninspired, I use premade herbal tea bags to flavor my meads. This is a wonderful way to achieve complexity in your short mead with minimum effort. I've found several brands of herbal iced tea blends that work beautifully for meads. One of my favorites is a hibiscus sangria iced tea blend that contains hibiscus, apple bits, sweet blackberry leaves, orange peel, orange, lemon, lime, and strawberry flavors. This particular blend is perfect for sipping on a hot summer evening. **Yield: *1 gallon***

- **1 large bag blended herbal tea or 2-3 small bags**
- **1.25 lb. honey**
- **1 gal. spring water or filtered, dechlorinated tap water**
- **¹⁄₁₆ tsp. yeast nutrient**
- **¼ package dry champagne yeast**

Instructions:

1. Place the yeast packet, stopper or lid, airlock, and scissors (to open the yeast packet) into a sanitizing solution. Clean and sanitize a glass jug.

2. Heat 2 cups of water to the appropriate temperature. A teapot is perfect for this purpose. Pour water over your tea bag(s), add yeast nutrient, and steep for 10 minutes. After 10 minutes, place your tea in a water bath to cool to below 75°F.

3. Place the jug on the scale. Zero the scale and add 1.25 pounds of honey.

4. Remove the jug from the scale, add filtered water, leaving enough room for the tea, cap or cover the opening securely, and shake until the honey and water are combined. Take a look at the bottom of your jug; if honey is still clinging on, keep shaking.

5. Uncap the jug and add the cooled tea.

6. Recap and shake to combine. Top off with water to bring up to 1 gallon if necessary. You may take a gravity reading using your hydrometer or refractometer at this point if you like. Your OG will be in the 1.040 to 1.046 range.

7. Uncap, pitch yeast, and place stopper or grommeted lid and airlock on jug.

8. Ferment between 66°F and 76°F for 5 to 14 days.

9. Taste after a week. If it's at your desired sweetness, package using the directions on pages 26 to 31. If it's too sweet, continue to taste every day or every other day until the mead is where you want. Higher fermentation temperatures will increase speed of fermentation. If you are taking gravity readings, I usually find 1.004 to 1.008 to be the ideal range.

Variations:

- **Coconut Custard Rooibos Short Mead:** I found a lovely coconut custard Rooibos loose tea blend at a local tea shop. I steeped 15 grams of the tea blend in 2 cups of off-boil water for 5 minutes, added my yeast nutrient, and proceeded as above. You can create your own coconut Rooibos tea by adding 5 grams of unsweetened dried coconut to 10 grams of Rooibos tea. Adjust to your liking.

- **Smoked Short Mead:** Create a smoky short mead by using lapsang souchong tea. Substitute 3 to 6 grams of lapsang souchong tea for the tea bags and use off-boil water for steeping. I find that lapsang souchong short meads take a bit longer to ferment out than other tea-based short meads.

CAFFEINATED TEA BLENDS

You can use herbal tea blends that contain green, white, or black tea as well, though they will likely end up more tannic than straight herbal blends. Treat these teas the same as herbal teas. I've also found some very interesting single-ingredient teas, including a spring spruce tip tea, that make lovely meads. Adjust the number of tea bags according to the strength of the tea and your preferences.

87

BOCHET

A short bochet is a lovely beverage on its own, showcasing the unique sweetness of honey. Decreasing or increasing the amount of time that you caramelize the honey can give you a range of flavors—similar to the variety that caramel candies come in. Caramelizing the honey before fermenting provides a depth of flavor that is a wonderful backdrop for other flavorings, especially dark fruits like plum and rich flavors like chocolate and peanut butter. **Yield: *1 gallon***

- **1.25 lb. honey**
- **1 gal. chilled spring water or filtered, dechlorinated chilled tap water**
- **¹⁄₁₆ tsp. yeast nutrient**
- **¼ package dry champagne yeast**

Instructions

1. Place the yeast packet, stopper or lid, airlock, and scissors (to open the yeast packet) into a sanitizing solution. Clean and sanitize a glass jug or jar.

2. Place a medium saucepan on the scale. Zero the scale and add 1.25 pounds of honey.

3. Heat the saucepan of honey over medium heat until boiling. Boil for 12 to 15 minutes, until a dark brown. Avoid burning your honey.

4. Cool the caramelized honey mixture slightly and add 4 to 5 cups chilled filtered water. Stir with a sanitized spoon to mix and take a temperature reading. Chill pan in an ice bath until below 75°F.

5. Add the caramelized honey mixture to your jug along with the beer yeast nutrients, top off with chilled water to 1 gallon, cap or cover the opening securely, and shake until the honey and water are combined. Take a look at the bottom of your jug; if honey is still clinging on, keep shaking.

6. You may take a gravity reading using your hydrometer or refractometer at this point if you like. Your OG will be in the 1.040 to 1.046 range.

7. Uncap, pitch yeast, and place stopper or grommeted lid and airlock on jug.

8. Ferment between 66°F and 76°F for 5 to 14 days.

9. Taste after a week. If it's at your desired sweetness, package using the directions on pages 26 to 31. If it's too sweet, continue to taste every day or every other day until

the mead is where you want. Higher fermentation temperatures will increase speed of fermentation. If you are taking gravity readings, I usually find 1.004 to 1.008 to be the ideal range.

Variations

- **Bananas Foster Short Bochet:** Heat 2 cups of freeze-dried bananas in ½ cup of dark rum in a saucepan over medium heat. Simmer until rum dissipates, stirring continuously. Add the softened banana mixture to the container after adding honey. Use sulfite-free dried banana chips for a variation (or if you can't find freeze-dried bananas).

- **Peanut Butter and Jelly Short Bochet:** Add ½ cup freeze-dried raspberries or strawberries and 1 tablespoon of powdered peanut butter to the container after adding the honey. You can substitute 2.5 cups of raw peanut shells, blanched in off-boil water for 5 minutes, instead of the powdered peanut butter.

- **Chocolate Pecan Pie Short Bochet:** Toast 1 cup of pecans in a medium saucepan over medium heat on the stovetop. Pat any excess oil off with a clean paper towel. Add toasted pecans along with 2 tablespoons roasted cocoa nibs and ½ teaspoon cocoa powder after adding honey to the jug or jar.

SHORT MEAD

CAPSICUMEL

Capsicumels are hot, in more ways than one. The first capsicumel that I tasted was a ghost pepper mead made by my friend Bob Slanzi. Bob went on to win Best of Show with his ghost pepper mead in New York City's biggest homebrew competition, beating out more than 750 beverages and becoming the first non-beer ever to nab that prize in the competition. He has now partnered with a commercial meadery to produce a line of hot pepper meads. Although Bob makes full-strength meads, hot peppers shine in short meads as well. We have an astounding variety of hot peppers available to us, and new varieties are being developed all the time. I recommend using restraint when brewing with chili peppers; once you've found a favorite, tweak your recipe to the level of heat you like. Capsicumels are a lovely foil for fruit additions as well. **Yield: *1 gallon***

- **1.25 lb. honey**
- **1 gal. chilled spring water or filtered, dechlorinated chilled tap water**
- **Chili pepper or peppers***
- **¹⁄₁₆ tsp. yeast nutrient**
- **¼ package dry champagne yeast**

Instructions

1. Place the yeast packet, stopper or lid, airlock, and scissors (to open the yeast packet) into a sanitizing solution. Clean and sanitize a glass jug or jar.
2. Bring water to a boil. A teapot is perfect for this. Pour ⅓ cup of off-boil water over the chilies and beer yeast nutrient and 2 to 3 cups of chilled filtered water to cool quickly.
3. Place your jug or jar on a kitchen scale. Zero the scale and add 1.25 pounds of honey.
4. Remove the jug from the scale, add filtered water, leaving enough room for the chili tea, cap or cover

*The amount of chili pepper used is highly dependent on the heat of the pepper as well as the spiciness desired. For example, 5 dried bird's-eye chilies in 1 gallon will give you a subtle warmth, but a sliver of the scorching scorpion pepper will do for 1 gallon of short mead. I avoid using the seeds in very hot chili peppers. When in doubt, use restraint. You can always add a chili tea at bottling if you would like to increase the heat.

the opening securely, and shake until the honey and water are combined. Take a look at the bottom of your jug; if honey is still clinging on, keep shaking.

5. Uncap the jug and add the cooled chili tea. Top off with water to reach 1 gallon, if necessary, and shake gently to blend.

6. You may take a gravity reading using your hydrometer or refractometer at this point if you like. Your OG will be in the 1.040 to 1.046 range.

7. Uncap, pitch yeast, and place stopper or grommeted lid and filled airlock on jug.

8. Ferment between 66°F and 76°F for 5 to 14 days.

9. Taste after a week. If it's at your desired sweetness, package using the directions on pages 26 to 31. If it's too sweet, continue to taste every day or every other day until the mead is where you want. Higher fermentation temperatures will increase speed of fermentation. If you are taking gravity readings, I usually find 1.004 to 1.008 to be the ideal range.

Variation

- **Cran-Habanero Short Mead:** Use ½ cup of freeze-dried cranberries and a quarter of a fresh habanero chili pepper.

ACERGLYN

This is a combination of two of my favorite natural sugar syrups, honey and maple syrup. The maple is most evident on the nose and complements the honey beautifully. I find that the darker, richer Grade B syrups work best in this beverage, fully expressing the maple character. I recommend bottling this a little earlier than other short meads to fully capture the sweet nature of the maple. This is a lovely beverage to drink with a weekend brunch, especially in the fall months. **Yield: *1 gallon***

- **15 oz. honey**
- **7 oz. maple syrup**
- **1 gal. chilled spring water or filtered, dechlorinated chilled tap water**
- **$1/16$ tsp. yeast nutrient**
- **$1/4$ package dry champagne yeast**

Instructions

1. Place the yeast packet, stopper or lid, airlock, and scissors (to open the yeast packet) into a sanitizing solution. Clean and sanitize a glass jug.

2. Place your jug or jar on a kitchen scale. Zero the scale and add 15 ounces of honey and 7 ounces of maple syrup.

3. Remove the jug from the scale, add filtered water to reach 1 gallon, cap or cover the opening securely, and shake until the honey, maple syrup, and water are combined. Take a look at the bottom of your jug; if syrup is still clinging on, keep shaking.

4. You may take a gravity reading using your hydrometer or refractometer at this point if you like. Your OG will be in the 1.042 to 1.048 range.

5. Uncap, pitch yeast, and place stopper or grommeted lid and filled airlock on jug.

6. Ferment between 66°F and 76°F for 5 to 14 days.

7. Taste after a week. If it's at your desired sweetness, package using the directions on pages 26 to 31. If it's too sweet, continue to taste every day or every other day until the mead is where you want. Higher fermentation temperatures will increase speed of fermentation. If you are taking gravity readings, I usually find 1.010 to 1.016 to be the ideal range.

DEVELOPING YOUR OWN SHORT MEAD

A SHORT MEAD is a high-quality blank canvas on which to paint with a full palette of flavors. I derive a lot of inspiration for short meads from tea blends, cocktail menus, and desserts—almost anything works well in a short mead, honestly. Begin building a new short mead recipe by considering the honey. You may wish to use a single-varietal honey, a seasonal blend, or a mixed floral blend. Just keep in mind that the aroma and flavor characteristics of the honey don't always translate when fermented into a short mead. It's often a good idea to do small half-gallon experiments (or even smaller) when using an expensive or rare honey for the first time. You can alter the honey character of your short mead by caramelizing the honey (making a bochet), using different yeasts, or packaging at a slightly higher final gravity—which will give you more residual honey aroma and flavor.

Next, consider your flavor additives. If you're combining flavorings such as fruit, herbal tea, herbs, and spices, make a tea with them first, adding a touch of honey for sweetening. Adjust the ratios of ingredients in the tea and use the same for your short mead. Keep in mind that it's always better to underseason than overseason—you can add a touch more tea at bottling if you desire more flavor. Try a couple of the recipes in this chapter and go from there. I bet you'll be sourcing local honey and scouring specialty tea shops and dessert recipe books in no time, concocting your own special short meads!

4

CITY CIDER

YOU WERE probably introduced to alcoholic cider as a sweet, mass-produced beverage. While I don't mind a pint of this type of cider occasionally, it's a far cry from many of the traditional ciders created around the world. Luckily, these drier traditional ciders are becoming more popular and accessible than ever.

My introduction to artisanal ciders came in 2001, when I read about an up-and-coming American cider maker in a food magazine. After I tracked it down, I took one sip and was completely captivated. This was nothing like the ciders I had tried before—it was dry, it was slightly tart, and it captured the beauty of that first bite of a fresh-picked apple in the fall. A trip to England cemented my love for this unique beverage, when I happened upon a cider stand at an outdoor market in London. I ordered a dry cider (in spite of the proprietor's warnings that it wasn't like American cider), and I savored every slightly tart sip as I browsed the market. A few days later I attended a traditional English cask festival and was introduced to a whole new world in the cider and perry corner. These were funky, earthy beverages with all kinds of depth, and I loved every one of them. I returned home and made my first batches of cider. Three gallons of fresh apple juice from the Green Market were divided into three gallon jugs: one got champagne yeast, one a *Brettanomyces-Saccharomyces* yeast blend, and the last a wild culture I had grown up from the skin of an organic apple also purchased at the market. I've never looked back!

CIDERS AROUND the WORLD

TRADITIONAL CIDERS were made from the juice of what we would consider inedible apples. They're tart, chalky, bitter and unpleasant in the mouth but ferment into a wonderfully complex beverage. These varieties of apples, high in acidity and tannins, are what drive the aroma and flavor of traditional ciders. Unfortunately, they've taken a backseat to the edible version in orchards in many parts of the world and can be difficult to find. You can source and press them at home, or you may be able to find fresh-pressed juice from traditional cider apples from a local artisanal cider maker. Homebrew stores are beginning to source fresh juice in the fall as well, and I encourage you to check availability with your local shop. However, you can also make wonderful cider at home using juice bought from your local grocery store or farmer's market. It's one of the simplest beverages to make; you simply pitch yeast into a jug of apple juice and let it ferment. The aroma and flavor of these ciders aren't dependent on the apples they are made from; the yeast and other additions, such as fruit, wood, and even hops, can create a wonderful array of delicious ciders to enjoy at home.

Although I'm lucky enough to be able to buy heirloom apple juice in my area, I enjoy making cider from store-bought juice just as much. Apples are a seasonal fruit, and fresh juice is available only for a limited amount of time, but prepackaged juice can be found year round. So while cider can be a unique beverage that showcases the beauty of locally produced fruit, it can also be an interesting base for other flavors.

Store-bought apple juice can be treated as a complementary base flavor or a neutral sugar source, depending on the yeast used and the other flavorings added. I view ciders as I do burgers: sometimes I start with the grass-fed organic beef patty, other times a veggie patty, and then I build from there. Sometimes it doesn't need anything; other times I stack it with cheese, bacon, a fried egg, the works. It's all delicious.

United Kingdom

Several different regions are known for their cider making, particularly the West Country and Kent. "Real" cider, cider made from 100 percent unpasteurized, unprocessed apple juice with traditional methods, is enjoying a comeback in the United Kingdom. Dry, medium, and sweet varieties of cider are produced, usually from a blend of apples, although single varietal ciders are made as well. They may be fermented naturally or with commercial yeasts, in wood barrels or stainless steel fermenters. English ciders vary in alcohol from 1.2 to 8.4 percent and range in aromas and flavors. West Country ciders tend to be drier and funkier, while ciders from the eastern areas tend to be sweeter.

France

The regions of Normandy and Brittany are best known for their *cidres*. French cidre making is often approached like wine making, using more intricate processes than other cider makers worldwide. Two varieties are common. Cidre Doux is a sweet style under 3 percent ABV that is typically produced through a complex process called keeving, while Cidre Brut is over 4.5 percent ABV and ranges in sweetness. Cidre is often sparkling and tends to

be drier, lighter-bodied, and more acidic than English varieties.

Spain

Most Spanish *sidra* comes from the north, in the Asturias and the Basque region. They're fermented from local apples with natural yeast and no processing. Most sidras are still (have no carbonation); are around 5 to 6 percent ABV; and are complex, with a musty, funky, slightly acetic character and a dry finish. They are often poured into the glass from great heights to aerate the sidra, giving the sensation of carbonation.

97

Canada

Cider was outlawed during the Canadian prohibition in the 1910s and didn't truly resurface until the late 1980s, when craft cideries were legalized. Ice cider, known as cidre de glace, was invented in the province of Quebec shortly thereafter, and cider has been gaining in popularity since. Ice cider is made from apples that have been frozen naturally and is typically between 9 and 13 percent ABV. Still and sparkling ciders with varying levels of alcohol are also made, as well as ciders flavored with local maple syrup, berries, and honey.

United States

Americans have a cider tradition that goes as far back as the first colonists. The Pilgrims brought apple seeds and cider making equipment with them to North America, and later John Chapman, fondly known as Johnny Appleseed, planted many an orchard across America, likely not for eating but for making cider. Apples picked from trees grown from seed are typically sour and considered inedible, but they make a very drinkable alcoholic cider. Unfortunately, many of these cider orchards were destroyed during Prohibition and the years following and were replaced with edible apple orchards. Artisanal cider resurfaced in the late 1990s and is now exploding. American cider makers are not only reviving traditional ciders but also taking cues from both international cider makers and craft brewers. Yep, not only are American cideries producing single heirloom varietal ciders and Spanish-style sidras but also flavored, dry-hopped, bourbon barrel–aged, and beer yeast–fermented ciders.

INGREDIENTS

Apple Juice

Look for apple juice that is free of additives and preservatives. You can use juice from a variety of sources: grocery stores, health food stores, farmers' markets, or your local orchard or cider maker. Containers labeled "100 percent apple juice" are best; avoid sulfites, sorbates, and benzoates, as they impair fermentation. Apple juices containing malic acid, citric acid, and ascorbic acid may be used but are less desirable than 100 percent juice.

If you're purchasing fresh locally pressed apple juice, ask if it is pasteurized and if so, what technique was used. If you find unpasteurized juice, it likely has a number of yeast and bacteria present. You can treat this in two ways: try to ferment it naturally or kill the existing bugs and ferment with a yeast of your choice. Fermenting naturally may produce an absolutely killer cider but is riskier. You are dealing with not only the natural yeast and bacteria on the fruit but also those that may be present on the pressing and packaging equipment. When I use fresh juice, I usually ferment a gallon naturally and treat the rest with commercial yeast. When using unpasteurized juice, you can eliminate the existing bugs by heating your cider or by using a form of potassium metabisulfite called Campden tablets. Heating your cider can drive away some flavor and aroma, so I find Campden tablets the better choice. Add one crushed Campden tablet per gallon of apple must, wait twenty-four to thirty-six hours, and pitch the commercial yeast of your choice. If you're buying pasteurized juice, ultraviolet (UV) pasteurization is the best choice, as it leaves more aroma and flavor than heat pasteurization does. Go with the flow; let your apple juice source help determine the type of cider you're making.

Beer Yeast Nutrient

Beer yeast nutrient will provide the yeast nutrition that the apple juice lacks.

Hops

The hops that brewers use to balance and add aroma and flavor to their beer are a wonderful addition to ciders. Whole hops and pellet hops may be used and can be found through homebrew suppliers. Please see the hops section in the beer chapter on pages 45 to 48 for a further exploration of hops.

Yeast

A variety of yeasts, wet or dry, may be used to create cider. The yeast used will impact the aroma, flavor, mouthfeel, and dryness of the resulting cider. On the next page is a chart containing the results of a cider yeast comparison that I conducted while

YEAST PITCHING QUANTITY	
Type of Yeast	**Pitching Quantity per 1 Gal. Cider**
Wet ale yeast	1/3 pack/packet/vial
Dry ale yeast	1/4 packet
Dry champagne yeast	1/3 packet

YEAST COMPARISON FOR CIDER

Yeast Type	Aroma Notes	Flavor Notes	Final Gravity (OG=1.044)
Champagne	Tart, clean, low to no apple aroma	Tart, low to medium apple flavor, dry, clean	1.002
American ale	Lots of apple, candy apple, sweet, blueberry, fruity	Fruity, sweet, apple medium to high, pineapple, blueberry	1.000
English ale	Green apple, bright, fruity, bubble gum, clean apple	Clean apple, bright, tart, sweet, green apple, mineral	1.004
German wheat	Sulfur, low to medium apple, honey, spicy	Phenolic, apple, applesauce, earthy	1.008
Belgian	Sulfur, funky, light apple, floral	Sulfur, floral, dry, funky, sweet-tart	1.000
Saison	Light apple, mineral, floral, herbal	Balanced, slight tartness, medium apple, floral, dry, tart	1.000

writing this book. Six half-gallon batches of apple juice were pitched with six different yeasts and fermented at 66°F for seven days. A panel of BJCP judges tasted the resulting ciders blindly and side-by-side and provided notes on aroma and flavor. Champagne, English ale, and saison were the judges' favorite yeasts.

Flavorings

You can affect the flavor of your cider by using any number of ingredients.

Fruit. Fruit is a great way to flavor your cider. Fresh or frozen fruit, frozen puree, freeze-dried fruit, and fruit juices all work well in cider. Regardless of the form, fruit and fruit juice free of additives and preservatives is recommended.

Herbs and spices. Both fresh and dried herbs and spices may be used. You can opt to add herbs and spices directly to the cider or make a tea first, with either apple juice or water as the base liquid.

HOW to MAKE CIDER

The following equipment and instructions are scaled for a 1-gallon batch size.

Materials
- 1-gal. jug or wide-mouth jar
- Sanitizer
- Long-handled, stainless-steel spoon
- Hydrometer
- Brewing notebook

Instructions

1. Clean and sanitize all equipment, including the 1-gallon jug or wide-mouth jar that will be used as the fermentation vessel.
2. If using dried herbs or spices, first make a tea by steeping herbs and spices in off-boil water for 10 to 15 minutes.
3. Add apple juice, flavorings, and/or tea to the 1-gallon jug or wide-mouth jar.
4. Stir with a sanitized spoon, or cap and shake to thoroughly combine.
5. Take a gravity reading, if desired.
6. Pitch yeast and ferment at 65°F to 70°F for 5 to 10 days.

101

CITY CIDER

This is the simplest of ciders—100 percent apple juice fermented with yeast. But the yeast you choose will make a significant difference in the resulting cider. Choose an American or English ale yeast for a sweeter cider with pronounced apple character, a white wine yeast for a drier cider with residual fruitiness, a champagne yeast for a dry cider, or even a saison yeast for an earthy, herbal cider. **Yield: *1 gallon***

- **1 gal. 100% apple juice**
- **Wet or dry yeast (see pitching chart on page 99)**
- **¹⁄₁₆ tsp. beer yeast nutrient**

Instructions

1. Add the juice and yeast nutrient to a sanitized 1-gallon jug or jar.
2. Take a gravity reading, if desired.
3. Pitch the yeast and top with a stopper or grommeted lid and filled airlock.
4. Ferment for 4 to 7 days at 65°F to 80°F.
5. Bottle as instructed on pages 26 to 31.

CULTURING YOUR OWN LOCAL YEAST and BACTERIA

I have cultured wild yeast and bacteria several times for use in fermenting cider. It's a bit more work, and riskier as far as results, but is a fun side project and definitely a conversation starter at homebrew meetings and parties. And you might end up with the best cider you have ever tasted! In the worst-case scenario, you don't like it, and you let it go to the best apple cider vinegar you've ever had. I have started with wild raspberries from my Brooklyn backyard and organic apples from the Green Market. You'll want to make a couple of starters to see if you get any activity.

The easiest method is to use a sanitized twelve- to twenty-ounce water or soda bottle; fill it one-third to halfway full with apple juice and add your yeast or bacteria source—either the actual fruit if it is small enough or the peel. Cap it and place it in a dark area between 65°F and 75°F. Check on it two to three times a day; once you see bubbling or foaming activity or the bottle begins to have less give when you press the sides, untwist the cap just enough to "burp" the bottle and take a whiff. If it's pleasant, you can start planning your cider. I typically let my starters go another twelve to twenty-four hours after activity first begins before using. Strain the fruit out and use the liquid as your yeast and bacteria, pitching as you normally would with a commercial yeast. If the starter smells unpleasant, don't use it—let it go to vinegar or discard it. I typically begin with two to four starters—I'm bound to have at least one turn out to be pitchable. You can use other containers as well; if you're using glass, use an airlock, and once it begins to bubble, uncap your vessel and take a whiff.

I prefer culturing from locally grown untreated or organic fruit, but you can also collect wild yeast and bacteria by placing juice in an open container; fasten some fabric over the top with a rubber band to keep out flies. Take advantage of your local yeast and bacteria; use a few different wild starters in half-gallon cider batches and see what happens. You can bottle them as-is or blend. Have fun!

CRANBERRY SPICE CIDER

This is a wonderful cider for fall festivities. It's beautiful paired with food or as a stand-alone sipper. Although cranberry juice blends are common, 100 percent cranberry juice can be a little tougher to find. Check local health food and gourmet stores if you don't see it on your local grocers' shelves. You can also cook down fresh cranberries, which are inexpensive and abundant in the fall months. I place fresh cranberries in a saucepan, add water to cover and simmer for 15 to 20 minutes. Cool slightly and strain the juice. You can use a variety of spices in this recipe; take inspiration from your favorite Thanksgiving cranberry recipe. I've added cloves to the mix, substituted orange peel for the lemon, and so forth. You could also substitute another juice for the cranberry—tart cherry would work beautifully. **Yield: *1 gallon***

- **15 c. 100% apple juice (1 c. short of 1 gal.)**
- **1¼ c. 100% cranberry juice**
- **2 star anise**
- **2 allspice berries**
- **½ stick cinnamon**
- **1 in. lemon peel (zest only, no pith)**
- **English ale yeast (see pitching chart on page 99)**
- **1/16 tsp. beer yeast nutrient**

Instructions

1. Place the spices in a microwaveable container and cover with ¼ cup of cranberry juice. Cover and microwave on high for 45 seconds. Remove and steep for 10 minutes.
2. Add the yeast nutrient and remaining cup of cranberry juice to sanitized 1-gallon jug or jar.
3. Strain out spices and add flavored juice to the container.
4. Add the apple juice to reach 1 gallon.
5. Stir with sanitized spoon, or cap and shake to combine.
6. Take a gravity reading, if desired.
7. Pitch the yeast and top with a stopper or grommeted lid and filled airlock.
8. Ferment for 4 to 7 days at 65°F to 80°F.
9. Bottle as instructed on pages 26 to 31.

TART BLACKBERRY CIDER

The combination of apple juice, blackberry puree, and champagne yeast adds up to a tart, refreshing drink reminiscent of a Berliner Weisse. Although it doesn't much resemble a traditional cider, this is one of my favorite ciders to make. This is a much more complex and interesting beverage than the simple list of ingredients would lead you to believe. **Yield: *1 gallon***

- **1 gal. 100% apple juice**
- **14 oz. frozen 100% blackberry pulp (found in Latin American or Mexican groceries)**
- **⅓ packet champagne yeast**
- **1/16 tsp. beer yeast nutrient**

Instruction

1. Thaw the blackberry pulp in the bag.

2. Add the yeast nutrient and thawed pulp to a sanitized 1-gallon jug or jar.

3. Add apple juice to reach 1 gallon.

4. Stir with sanitized spoon, or cap and shake to combine.

5. Take a gravity reading, if desired.

6. Pitch the yeast and top with a stopper or grommeted lid and filled airlock.

7. Ferment for 4 to 7 days at 65°F to 80°F.

8. Bottle as instructed on pages 26 to 31.

DRY-HOPPED CIDER

Cider loves hops. I was blown away by the results of my hopped cider experiments. Cider expresses the unique aroma and flavor of hops beautifully—particularly the juicy, fruity varieties. This is such a simple process, and it has become one of my go-to fast-fermented beverages to make for parties and other celebrations. My personal favorite hops to use are Nelson Sauvin and Citra, but I have yet to meet an aroma hop that cider doesn't like. While ciders display single hop varieties to perfection, blends are an option as well. This is a wonderful drink for anyone who loves the aroma and flavor of hops, particularly those with an aversion to the bitterness of hoppy beers or an intolerance to gluten. Use an American or English ale yeast if you'd like more sweetness and apple character or a champagne yeast for a drier, more neutral cider. **Yield: *1 gallon***

- **1 gal. 100% apple juice**
- **¼ oz. hop pellets (single variety or a blend)**
- **⅓ packet champagne yeast**
- **¹⁄₁₆ tsp. beer yeast nutrient**

Instructions

1. Add the apple juice and yeast nutrient to a sanitized 1-gallon jug or jar.
2. Take a gravity reading, if desired.
3. Pitch the yeast and top with a stopper or grommeted lid and filled airlock.
4. Ferment for 4 to 7 days at 65°F to 80°F.
5. Add hop pellets and rest at 32°F to 40°F for 2 days. (A refrigerator works well for this.)
6. Bottle as instructed on pages 26 to 31.

NOT-SO-DARK-AND-STORMY CIDER

Once upon a time, I took a crazy little trip to Bermuda and fell in love with a drink called Dark 'n' Stormy. That combination of spicy ginger beer and black rum was irresistible. I found myself trying to capture those fascinating flavors in a fermented, low-alcohol beverage. I didn't reach the darkness that I anticipated, but this turned out to be one fine drink. This is like a summer daytime thunderstorm—entrancing, electrifying, and dangerous in its drinkability. **Yield:** *1 gallon*

- **1 gal. 100% apple juice**
- **½ c. filtered water**
- **8 g cinnamon stick**
- **½ tsp. anise seed**
- **2 in. vanilla bean, insides scraped**
- **1 oz. grated fresh ginger**
- **1 tbsp. dark molasses**
- **¼ packet English ale yeast or ⅓ packet champagne yeast**
- **¹⁄₁₆ tsp. beer yeast nutrient**

Instructions

1. Bring ½ cup of filtered, chlorine-free water to a boil.
2. Pour the ½ cup of off-boil water over the spices and steep for 10 minutes.
3. Strain out spices and add the tea and yeast nutrient to a sanitized 1-gallon container.
4. Add apple juice to reach 1 gallon.
5. Stir with sanitized spoon, or cap and shake to combine.
6. Take a gravity reading, if desired.
7. Pitch the yeast and top with a stopper or grommeted lid and filled airlock.
8. Ferment for 4 to 7 days at 65°F to 80°F.
9. Bottle as instructed on pages 26 to 31.

CHERRY "BOURBON-AGED" CIDER

This cider takes a cue from barrel-aged ciders. While you won't get the full impact of a true barrel-aged cider, this version is too simple and delicious to resist. The cherry juice and bourbon-soaked oak chips complement the cider character and add complexity. This one is also crying for variations. You may substitute other juices or fruit pulp for the cherry juice and other liquors for the bourbon. And there are a variety of other wood chips available from homebrew and smoker suppliers. **Yield: *1 gallon***

- **15 c. 100% apple juice (1 c. short of 1 gal.)**
- **1 c. 100% tart cherry juice**
- **1 tbsp. bourbon-soaked light toast oak chips***
- **¼ packet English ale yeast or ⅓ packet champagne yeast**
- **¹⁄₁₆ tsp. beer yeast nutrient**

Instructions

1. Add the cherry juice and yeast nutrient to a sanitized 1-gallon jug or jar.
2. Add apple juice to reach 1 gallon.
3. Add ½ tablespoon of bourbon-soaked oak chips (drained of bourbon).
4. Stir with sanitized spoon, or cap and shake to combine.
5. Take a gravity reading, if desired.
6. Pitch the yeast and top with a stopper or grommeted lid and filled airlock.
7. Ferment for 4 to 7 days at 65°F to 80°F.
8. Bottle as instructed on pages 26 to 31.

*To prepare oak chips: Boil oak chips for 5 to 10 minutes in enough water to cover. Drain and spread on baking sheet to dry. After fully dry, place in small glass jar and add bourbon to cover. Soak for a minimum of 24 hours before using in your fermentation. I keep four small jars of oak chips on hand at all times: one with rum, one with bourbon, one with rye, and one with a smoky whiskey.

DRY LAVENDER CIDER

Lavender is a polarizing flavor, particularly in beverages. I happen to love it, and this cider is a delightful expression of the unique aroma and flavor of lavender. I find that dry saison yeast emphasizes the floral, perfumed quality of the lavender. If you're not a lavender lover, substitute another herb that you love; rosemary, thyme, lemon verbena, and other aromatic herbs are lovely in this cider. **Yield: *1 gallon***

- **1 gal. 100% apple juice**
- **2 tsp. dried lavender**
- **¼ packet dry saison yeast**
- **¹⁄₁₆ tsp. beer yeast nutrient**

Instructions

1. Add the juice and yeast nutrient to a sanitized 1-gallon jug or jar.
2. Blanch the lavender by dipping into boiling water. Follow by dipping into ice water.
3. Add lavender to apple juice.
4. Take a gravity reading, if desired.
5. Pitch the yeast and top with a stopper or grommeted lid and filled airlock.
6. Ferment for 4 to 7 days at 65°F to 80°F.
7. Bottle as instructed on pages 26 to 31.

DEVELOPING YOUR OWN CITY CIDER

CIDER IS MAKING a comeback worldwide. For good reason—it's delicious, historic, and one of the simplest, most natural fermented beverages to make. And although I love traditional ciders dearly, the new wave of ciders using nontraditional ingredients has won me over. Whether you choose to make a cider from fresh-pressed heirloom apples, in a style from another part of the world, or with nouveau ingredients, have fun and revel in the true beauty that is cider.

Ciders are an excellent neutral yet natural foundation when using champagne yeast yet can add apple character and residual sweetness when using an American or English ale yeast. And ciders are one of the easiest beverages to ferment, requiring minimal time and materials. They showcase a myriad of ingredients, from fruit to hops to herbs and spices. I enjoy taking inspiration from cocktail menus, commercial ciders, tea blends, and apple-based dishes, to name just a few. Tap into your creative side and see what happens! I have a list a mile long of City Cider recipe ideas for future batches: caramel apple cider, smoked apple cider, Waldorf apple cider, peanut butter apple cider, coconut apple cider, carrot apple cider . . . the list goes on!

5

BOOZY BUCH & KEFIR BEER

WHEN I STARTED to write this chapter, I was sitting in one of my favorite beer bars in the Williamsburg neighborhood of Brooklyn, enjoying a pint. But it wasn't a pint of craft beer or cider, which they have aplenty; it was a pint of kombucha. This particular kombucha had been made less than a mile and half from where I sat, and it was absolutely delicious—tart, thirst-quenching, and less than 0.5 percent alcohol. That meant I could keep a clear head while I wrote and still enjoy an amazingly satisfying beverage.

Drinks like kombucha and water kefir are perfect to have between beers when you're out for the evening with friends, and it's just plain delicious if you're looking for a nonalcoholic alternative to your favorite beer, cider, cocktail, or wine. They're chock-full of probiotics (live organisms, such as bacteria and yeast, that are believed to be beneficial to your health), can be flavored in endless ways, and are dead easy and dirt-cheap to brew at home. The other benefit of brewing your own at home is that both are easy to turn into alcoholic beverages.

ABOUT BUCH, KEFIR & BOOZE

SOUR BEER IS one of my favorite styles of beer to drink and to brew, but aside from sour-mashed and kettle-soured versions (page 68), they're quite tricky to make. Besides being unpredictable, they often take up to several years to produce, tying up your fermentation vessels and taking up space in your living quarters. They can also be quite expensive; mixed yeast and bacteria cultures, flavorings, and wood/barrel costs all add up. I've found that boozy kombucha is a great alternative for us sour beer lovers—especially when we're pressed for time or simply don't want to wait a year or more to drink what we've brewed. Boozy buch is a fantastically tart, flavorful, and complex alcoholic drink. Plus, you can blend it with other beverages—beer, cider, short mead, and more—to add complexity and a touch of tartness. Oh, and it's easy and quick to brew, of course!

Kombucha

Kombucha has been around quite a while; the first record of it dates back to 220 BCE in what is now northeastern China. Essentially, kombucha begins as a sweet tea and is fermented using a mushroom-shaped symbiotic culture of yeast and bacteria, or SCOBY (seen at right). The SCOBY is composed of a number of bacteria (primarily *Acetobacter* varieties) and yeast (*Saccharomyces* and *Brettanomyces* among them) that symbiotically form a cellulosic biofilm. This matrix is what gives the rubbery, somewhat slimy SCOBY its

shape and form. Kombucha SCOBYs are quite unique; they are thick, gelatinous, opaque masses in shades of cream, tan, and brown. They're usually round, as they take the shape of the container in which they are fermented. The first time I saw one, it reminded me of an alien life form!

To make kombucha, a SCOBY is placed in a container of sweet tea and allowed to ferment at room temperature. The yeast breaks down the sucrose into glucose and fructose, creating ethanol and carbon dioxide, and the bacteria converts the glucose into gluconic acid and fructose into acetic acid. Some of the ethanol is also converted to acetic acid. Several other compounds may be produced, including lactic acid and a range of aromatic and flavor compounds. Finished kombucha is tart, with a pH generally between 2.4 and 2.8, and may range in alcohol content from less than 0.5 percent to over 2 percent, depending on the yeast and bacteria mixture as well as fermentation conditions. Kombucha typically takes anywhere between four days and two weeks for primary fermentation. Flavorings may be added to kombucha during a secondary fermentation or at bottling.

Once primary fermentation is finished, the SCOBY is removed and reused to ferment a new batch. SCOBYs grow over time, producing "babies" that can be peeled off and used in new batches. SCOBYs can also be cut up and used in multiple batches, as they will grow to the shape and size of the container over time. If treated properly, SCOBYs may be reused indefinitely.

Water Kefir

Water kefir is another delicious, nonalcoholic alternative, similar to a natural soda. Even faster to ferment than kombucha, it showcases flavors to a tee and is inexpensive and simple to brew at home. Also like kombucha, it can be turned into a delicious alcoholic beverage, which I like to call kefir beer.

Also known as tibicos, it has a somewhat murky history, but it was first noted in the 1890s and is thought to originate in Mexico, Tibet, southern Ukraine, or the Caucasus Mountains. It's a bit of a mystery, kind of like the culture itself. Note that there is a separate but related kefir culture that is used to ferment dairy, commonly called milk kefir.

Water kefir begins as a sugar solution and is fermented with gelatinous SCOBY chunks commonly called grains (pictured on the next page). The grains usually contain more than 450 bacterial strains

nutrients and fermented at room temperature. The nutrients can range from sea salt to eggshells to baking soda to fruit. The yeast break down the sucrose into glucose and fructose, creating ethanol and carbon dioxide, and the bacteria converts the glucose primarily into lactic acid, although ethanol and acetic acid may be produced. Aroma and flavor compounds are produced as well. Water kefir has a very fast turnover, completing primary fermentation in less than forty-eight hours. Flavorings may be added in primary fermentation, secondary fermentation, or when bottling. Water kefir may have a slight lactic tartness that is balanced by residual sugar, and it is generally around 0.5% ABV or less, although it may go higher under certain conditions. The grains will generally multiply with time and when treated properly, may be reused indefinitely.

Kombucha SCOBYs and water kefir grains have not been studied extensively; as they are open-fermented, they likely mutate over time, as has been documented with other open-fermented cultures like sourdough. They are wild cultures and are therefore less predictable and controllable than commercial yeast and bacteria cultures. The bacterial and yeast components in a kombucha SCOBY or cluster of water

and four strains of yeast. *Lactobacillus* varieties are the most common type of bacteria found in water kefir grains, with *Acetobacter*, *Streptococcus*, *Pediococcus*, *Leuconostoc*, and a few others present as well. These hang together in a polysaccharide matrix. Instead of forming a thick pancake like a kombucha SCOBY, the culture forms translucent jelly clusters that have a crushed-ice shape.

To make water kefir, the grains are placed in a simple syrup along with kefir grains may differ from one culture to the next. This is not meant to frighten those of you who have mastered brewing with commercial yeast, but to let you know that an open mind and sense of adventure will take you far in your kombucha and water kefir brewing.

Adding the Alcohol

Okay, so what about the boozy versions? Once you have a finished batch of water kefir or kombucha, you simply mix in additional sugar, flavorings, and rehydrated champagne yeast, then cap your vessel, add an airlock, and ferment into a tasty intoxicating drink. It's that easy.

Yes, that first fermentation is an additional step over every other beverage in this book, but it adds a whole layer of complexity that you can't obtain otherwise. Remember, this is a simple way to get a sour adult beverage—and those typically take so much longer! Kombucha and water kefir also have the ability to capture aromas and flavors that are tricky to obtain in other beverages; for example, strawberries are notoriously difficult to capture in a beer but are easily expressed in water kefir. And boozy buch and water kefir

JUN

Jun is a relative of kombucha that ferments honey and green tea instead of sugar and black tea. Jun SCOBYs are similar in appearance to those used for kombucha but tend to be lighter in color. The resulting beverage is less acidic than kombucha, making for a complex but slightly smoother beverage. Jun is a nice alternative to kombucha for those who are sensitive to acetic notes. Jun SCOBYs are rarer than kombucha SCOBYs, but can be purchased through online vendors.

retain body and mouthfeel even when fermented to a very low final gravity, unlike a cider, short mead, or spirited soda. Finally, these beverages are rare to nonexistent in the marketplace. Although there are over eighty kombucherys in the United States and Canada, only a few are making alcoholic kombucha. And I haven't found a single alcoholic water kefir produced commercially. These are exciting and enticing beverages that beg for exploration—here's to a new adventure in brewing!

INGREDIENTS

Kombucha SCOBY

Look locally for your SCOBY first. You may be able to obtain a kombucha SCOBY at no cost from a friend or acquaintance who makes kombucha. Ask around or post a request via your favorite social media; you may be surprised how many of your friends are already brewing kombucha. There are online fermentation groups that maintain lists of locally available cultures, or perhaps you have a kombuchery in your area; reach out to see if they sell or give away SCOBYs. If you can't find a SCOBY locally, you can purchase one from a number of online retailers. SCOBYs can come in a wet or dehydrated from. Regardless of the form, it may take a couple of batches before your SCOBY reaches its full potency.

Water Kefir Grains

These may be a bit more difficult to obtain locally than a kombucha SCOBY, as they aren't quite as popular. Ask your friends, post a request on social media, and search online fermentation boards. If you can't find a local source for water kefir grains, there are several online sources. You can purchase these fresh or dried. Regardless of your source, your grains may not reach their full fermentation capacity for a few cycles.

Filtered Water

I use water that has been run through a simple under-sink charcoal filter, which removes the chlorine as well as other impurities. Removing the chlorine is essential.

Sugars

Refined white sugar is best for primary kombucha fermentations, as this is what they are accustomed to fermenting. You can train your SCOBY to feed on other sugars, but this should be done over time and can be tricky. A variety of sugars may be used in the secondary fermentation when you add your commercial yeast.

Water kefir grains are typically accustomed to refined sugar. Adding a small portion of less-refined sugars can add flavor as well as nutrients. You can train your grains to grow on other sugar sources, but like kombucha SCOBYs, this takes time and can be unpredictable. You can use a variety of sugars in your secondary fermentation with commercial yeast.

For more on sugars, refer to pages 13 to 16.

Yeast

Champagne yeast is the ideal choice for kombucha and kefir because it not only tolerates a wide range of fermentation temperatures but also ferments in low-pH conditions. Rehydrating with Go-Ferm (see below) before adding the yeast to the kombucha helps ensure that it is able to fully ferment in a challenging acidic environment full of competitive bacteria and yeast. I've experimented with ale yeasts but have found that they produce off-aromas and flavors when making boozy buch and kefir beer, so I recommend champagne yeast for the beverages in this chapter.

Go-Ferm and Go-Ferm Protect

Go-Ferm is a yeast rehydration nutrient that is added to the water when rehydrating dry yeast. Go-Ferm will give your commercial yeast a healthy start and ensure that it has the nutrients it needs to ferment fully. Because we are adding commercial yeast to a broth full of bacteria and yeast, the Go-Ferm will help ensure that the commercial yeast receive the nutrients more so than the bacteria and yeast already present in the kombucha or water kefir. Go-Ferm also helps give the commercial yeast an edge in the acidic kombucha broth.

Clockwise from top left: cranberries, brown sugar, hop pellets, pink Himalayan salt, white sugar.

Hops

Hops are a wonderful addition to kefir beers and kombucha. Please see pages 45 to 48 for detailed information on hops. Hops can be purchased through local or online homebrew suppliers.

Nutrients

These will be added sparingly in 100 percent white sugar primary water kefir fermentations and can range from molasses, mineral-rich salts such as sea salt or pink Himalayan salt, eggshells, unsulfured dried fruit, or beer yeast nutrients. My standard nutrient addition for primary water kefir fermentation is pink Himalayan salt, which I purchase in bulk from a local warehouse store.

Teas

Kombucha primary fermentation is always built on a tea substrate, but you can also add tea to your secondary fermentations in both beverages (see the chart on pages 124 to 125).

Kombucha SCOBYs thrive on real tea—the leaves picked from the *Camellia sinensis* plant—as it provides the minerals and nitrogen kombucha SCOBYs require. Real teas include black tea, oolong, green, white and pu'erh. The difference among these types is a reflection of the fermentation and oxidation that the leaves go through after being picked. Herbal teas may be used in combination with real tea. I've also used flavored teas, although these may be detrimental to your SCOBY over time, particularly if they contain oils, and are best used in secondary fermentation. I recommend beginning with black tea and mixing in other teas as you feel more confident about the process. My standard tea blend for primary kombucha fermentation when making a boozy buch is a blend of half black tea and half green and white

tea. Keep in mind that fermentation does not decrease the caffeine content of your tea; the amount of caffeine in your initial tea will be the amount of caffeine in your finished beverage. If you get crazy with your tea blends and notice your SCOBY is looking a little worse for wear, go back to straight black tea for a few batches.

Flavorings

Fruits, herbs, spices, and teas all work well in flavoring kombucha and water kefir. Both beverages will have developed aroma and flavor compounds during primary fermentation, and you'll want to select flavors that work well with these. Kombucha has an acetic backbone, so you'll want to choose flavors that work well in a sour beverage. Water kefir typically has a softer lactic tartness but a gentle earthy roundness. You may wish to build on the sourness in both beverages by using tart fruits like rhubarb, or you can contrast with earthier flavorings like coriander. You can build complexity by combining fruits, herbs, and spices. Browse kombuchery web sites for flavor inspiration.

Fruits. Fresh, dried, and freeze-dried fruit and fruit juice all work well in both fermentations. Although they can be added to the primary fermentation, they work best in secondary fermentation when you add your commercial yeast.

Herbs and spices. Fresh or dried herbs and spices can add zing to your kombucha and water kefir.

EQUIPMENT

Fermentation Vessels

Wide-mouth jars ranging from a quart to a gallon are available at homebrew stores as well as dollar, discount, and variety stores. Food-grade plastic pails or buckets may also be used and are available at restaurant supply stores. Stainless steel is acceptable as well, but aluminum and other reactive metal containers are not recommended.

Funnels

A wide-mouth funnel and a narrow-mouth funnel made of plastic, silicone, or stainless steel are recommended. It's helpful (but not necessary) to have a variety of sizes.

Strainers

It helps to have a variety of sizes of fine-mesh plastic strainers. The type that are sold in three-packs at discount stores are perfect.

Teapot

A saucepan may be used, but a teapot is ideal for heating water to make teas for your kombucha.

Heat-Tolerant Pitcher

You'll need a heat-tolerant pitcher that holds four or more cups for making teas in. You can use a nonreactive metal or glass saucepan, but a container with a pouring spout is ideal.

Tea Infuser or Fillable Tea Bags

If you use loose tea, place your tea in a tea infuser or disposable tea bags. You can make your own disposable tea bags easily from paper coffee filters.

Covers for Your Jars

Primary water kefir and kombucha fermentations are open fermentations. A piece of lightweight fabric and rubber bands or elastic will keep out the fruit flies and other

(continued on page 126)

TEA CHART

Type of Tea	What Is It?
Black	Fully oxidized tea leaves: black tea leaves are withered, rolled, then allowed to ferment and oxidize fully. The leaves are then heated to stop further oxidation.
Oolong	Partially oxidized tea leaves: oolong tea leaves are withered, rolled, then fermented to partial oxidation. The leaves are then heated to stop further oxidation.
Green	Nonoxidized tea leaves: green tea leaves are heated, rolled, and dried immediately after being picked, preventing fermentation and oxidation.
White	The least processed of all real teas: white tea leaves are carefully dried without added heat to produce a delicate, unfermented, nonoxidized tea.
Pu'erh	Pu'erh is green tea that has undergone a secondary fermentation of at least 6 months.
Yerba mate	Leaves from the yerba mate plant, a form of holly, are dried, shredded, and aged for a year in cedar containers. They contain a variety of vitamins.
Rooibos	Rooibos is caffeine-free herbal tea from the Rooibos, or red bush plant.
Herbal	Herbal teas are other leaves, fruits, bark, roots, or flowers used to make tea, usually caffeine-free. Examples include chamomile, mint, and hibiscus.
Flavored tea	Flavored tea is any tea that has added natural or artificial flavorings or oils.

Use in Kombucha	Aroma/Flavor Notes	Ideal Steeping Temperature
May be used 100%	Apple, wood, earth, leather, dark chocolate, raisins, berries, licorice	195–205°F
May be used 100%	Wide array: grass, orchid, peach, tropical fruit, honey, citrus, butter, mineral, coconut, melon, wood	195°F
May be used 100% but commonly blended with black teas	Fresh-cut grass, cucumber, bamboo, kale, floral, melon, vanilla, spinach	175°F
Best blended with at least 15% black, oolong, or green tea	Floral, honey, apricot, vanilla, light wood, honeysuckle, honeydew	175°F
May be used 100%	Earth, dark chocolate, licorice, molasses, leather, espresso, pecans, mushroom	195–205°F
Need to blend with at least 25% black, oolong, or green tea	Smoke, grass, herbal	208°F
Need to blend with at least 25% black, oolong, or green tea	Honey, wood, spice, caramel, herbal, floral	208°F
Need to blend with at least 25% black, oolong, or green tea	Varies	208°F
Unsuitable for primary fermentation; excellent for flavoring in secondary fermentation	Varies	Steeping temperature for base tea

My loft gets very chilly in the winter, dropping to the 50s°F by January. I built a simple fermentation chamber for my warmth-loving fermentations with insulated foam board and a grow mat with a thermo-regulator attached.

You can even use a cardboard box or a wooden crate with a low-watt light bulb inside. If you have the opposite temperature issue, you can keep your fermentations cool in extreme heat using a cooler filled with ice packs and water.

critters but allow your fermentations to breathe. You can cut up an old lightweight T-shirt or use scraps of muslin. You can even substitute paper towels for the fabric in a pinch. Ideally, your fabric cover should extend at least two inches beyond the circumference of your jar to make it easier to secure the band around the top.

Cleanser

Dish soap and hot water suffice for primary fermentation, but brewing cleansers or oxygenated powdered cleanser are ideal.

Sanitizer

I recommend cleaning and sanitizing your supplies and equipment the same way you would for brewing beer. Although you're beginning your boozy buch and kefir beer batch with an unsanitized mixed yeast and bacteria broth, sanitizing will keep out other unwanted microbes and ensure that you begin with the mixed culture that you've already developed.

pH Meter or pH Test Strips

A pH meter or pH strips are optional but helpful in determining the pH of your kombucha and water kefir. Both kombucha and water kefir fermentation is quite temperature sensitive, and obtaining a pH reading can help determine when your kombucha is ready to be drunk or fermented into an alcoholic beverage.

PRIMARY KOMBUCHA FERMENTATION

Use this recipe as a base for the recipes on pages 130 and 132, or see page 139 for some ideas on how to start your own kombucha explorations. **Yield: *1 gallon***

- **1 kombucha SCOBY**
- **1 gal. spring water or filtered, dechlorinated tap water**
- **6 regular-size tea bags or 12 g loose tea, placed in a disposable tea bag or infuser**
- **1 c. white sugar**
- **1 c. starter tea (from a previous batch of kombucha) or 2 tbsp. white vinegar**

Instructions

1. Bring 2 cups of water to just boiling. Pour the water over the tea bags or tea infuser in a heat-resistant pitcher or saucepan. Stir and steep for 15 to 20 minutes.

2. Once the tea has steeped, add 1 cup of sugar and 2 to 4 cups of water and stir to mix thoroughly. The amount of water will depend on the temperature of the water; you want the final mixture to be below 85°F. You can even use ice made from chlorine-free water for this.

3. Add the sweet tea mixture to a clean wide-mouth gallon jar along with a cup of fermented kombucha (from a previous batch or purchased) or 2 tablespoons of white vinegar. The addition of starter tea or vinegar brings the solution to more favorable pH range for the SCOBY.

4. Top off with water, leaving enough room for the SCOBY.

5. Stir to combine, ensuring that all of the sugar has dissolved.

6. Add the SCOBY to the sweet tea mixture and rubber-band the fabric over the top. The SCOBY may float, sink to the bottom, or end up somewhere in between.

7. Ferment out of direct sunlight between 68°F and 85°F (ideally 70°F to 80°F) for 4 days to 2 weeks. The kombucha will ferment faster in warmer temperatures and will slow down considerably below 66°F. You risk developing mold if the temperatures are too low or harsh and unpalatable flavors if they are too high. If you have a pH meter or pH strips, the pH of finished kombucha is generally between 2.7 and 3.1.

PRIMARY WATER KEFIR FERMENTATION

Use this recipe as a base for the recipes on pages 134 and 136, or see page 139 for some ideas on how to start your own water kefir explorations. **Yield: *1 gallon***

- **6–8 tbsp. water kefir grains**
- **1 gal. spring water or filtered, dechlorinated tap water**
- **1 c. white sugar or ¾ c. white sugar and ¼ cup less-processed sugar**
- **Nutrients (choose one if using 100% white sugar): pinch of sea salt or Himalayan salt, clean eggshell, unsulfured dried fruit (equivalent to 1–2 apricots or prunes or 6–8 raisins), pinch of beer yeast nutrient, or 1 tbsp. molasses**

Instructions

1. Add the sugar or sugars to a clean wide-mouth gallon jar.
2. If using 100 percent white sugar, add the nutrients.
3. Top with water, leaving enough room for the water kefir grains, and stir thoroughly to combine. Make sure that all of the sugar has dissolved into solution.
4. Add the grains to the jar of sugar solution and cover the top with fabric, securing with a rubber band or piece of elastic. The grains will likely sink to the bottom, but some may float at the top or hover somewhere in between.
5. Ferment out of direct sunlight in temperatures between 65°F and 82°F for 24 to 48 hours. You risk developing mold if the temperatures are too low or developing harsh and unpalatable flavors and damage to your grains if the temperatures are too high. The kefir will taste less sweet and have other flavors develop when it is finished. If you have a pH meter or pH strips, the pH of finished water kefir is generally between 3.0 and 4.5.

TAKING A KOMBUCHA or WATER KEFIR VACATION

If you'd like to take a break from kombucha brewing, make a new batch and place it in a secure, dark location. Your SCOBY will keep for quite awhile at normal room temperatures. You will need to add about ¼ cup of sugar or replace some of the kombucha with fresh sweet tea every four to six weeks. If you would like to take an extended break, you may keep your SCOBY in a sealed plastic bag or glass container in your refrigerator in a fresh batch of sweet tea with starter culture added. Note that it may take your SCOBY a few batches to return to normal fermentation strength after spending time at refrigerator temperatures.

If you'd like to take a break from water kefir brewing, make a small batch of sugar solution (¼ cup of sugar to one quart of water), add the grains, seal in a glass jar with a lid, and place in the refrigerator. This will keep for two to four weeks. If you would like to take an extended break, simply change the sugar solution every two to four weeks. Note that it may take the water kefir grains a few batches to return to normal fermentation strength after spending time at refrigerator temperatures.

TART CHERRY BOOZY BUCH

Tart cherries are one of my favorite flavorings for boozy buch. The tartness of the fruit complements the sourness of the kombucha, and the sweetness adds balance. Sweet cherries work just as well, however. I stock up on fresh local cherries during the season and freeze them to use throughout the year. You can also use dried cherries, freeze-dried cherries, cherry puree, or cherry juice. Avoid anything containing preservatives. This is also lovely with flavorings such as almond, Rooibos, or vanilla. **Yield:** *1 gallon*

- **1 gal. fermented kombucha (see page 127)**
- **½ c. sugar**
- **1 c. fresh or frozen tart cherries, washed and thawed**
- **½ packet champagne yeast**
- **1 tsp. Go-Ferm (approximately 3 g)**
- **¹/₁₆ tsp beer yeast nutrient**

Instructions

1. Hydrate the yeast with Go-Ferm. Heat ¼ cup water to 104°F. Stir in 1 teaspoon of Go-Ferm and sprinkle ½ packet of champagne yeast on top. Let stand for 20 minutes.
2. Add the cherries to a sanitized 1-gallon wide-mouth jar.
3. Remove the SCOBY and 1 cup of fermented kombucha from the container and set them aside in a clean container (a shallow bowl is perfect). Strain the fermented kombucha into the jar, capturing any stray SCOBY material in the mesh strainer. Discard the material in the strainer.
4. Add a dash of beer yeast nutrient and stir gently to combine.
5. You may take a gravity reading using your hydrometer or refractometer at this point if you choose. Your OG will be in the 1.030 to 1.034 range, although this will depend on how much sugar remained in your fermented kombucha. You may add more sugar at this time if you would like a higher starting gravity. I do not recommend going over 1.040 when you are beginning boozy buch brewing.
6. Add the rehydrated yeast solution.
7. Seal your jar with a grommeted lid or stopper and filled airlock.

8. Use the SCOBY and reserved kombucha to begin a new batch of kombucha, using the directions for primary kombucha fermentation on page 127.

9. Ferment your boozy buch between 68°F and 80°F for 7 to 14 days, until desired taste is obtained.

10. Bottle as directed on pages 26 to 31.

Variations

- **Cherry-Almond-Rooibos Boozy Buch:** Boil ½ cup of water. Pour off-boil water over 2 almond-Rooibos tea bags and steep for 10 to 15 minutes. Add strained tea when adding cherries.

- **Mango Boozy Buch:** Substitute ½ cup honey for the sugar and 6 to 8 frozen mango chunks for the cherries. Thaw before using.

SPEARMINT BOOZY BUCH

Mint and kombucha seem like a strange flavor combination to me, and I'll admit that I was a little surprised to find out how well they go together. Spearmint Boozy Buch is lively, smooth, and oh-so-refreshing—my favorite for summer. Flavoring boozy buches is one of my favorite ways to use all of those fancy flavored teas that tempt me whenever I go into a specialty tea store. Honestly, I like flavored teas in boozy buch better than I like them steeped as tea; the carbonation and tart background add a whole new dimension. Tea-flavored buches are superfun, supersimple, and superdelicious to make! **Yield: *1 gallon***

- **1 gal. fermented kombucha (see page 127)**
- **½ c. sugar**
- **½ c. filtered water**
- **4 g dried spearmint or 2 spearmint tea bags**
- **½ packet champagne yeast**
- **1 tsp. Go-Ferm (approximately 3 g)**
- **¹⁄₁₆ tsp beer yeast nutrient**

Instructions

1. Hydrate the yeast with Go-Ferm. Heat ¼ cup water to 104°F. Stir in 1 teaspoon of Go-Ferm and sprinkle ½ packet of champagne yeast on top. Let stand for 20 minutes.

2. Bring ½ cup of water to a boil. Pour the off-boil water over the dried spearmint or tea bags and steep for 10 to 15 minutes. Strain and add to a sanitized 1-gallon jar or jug.

3. Remove the SCOBY and 1 cup of fermented kombucha from the container and set them aside in a clean container (a shallow bowl is perfect). Strain the fermented kombucha into the jar, capturing any stray SCOBY material in the mesh strainer. Discard the material in the strainer.

4. Add a dash of beer yeast nutrient and stir gently to combine.

5. You may take a gravity reading using your hydrometer or refractometer at this point if you choose. Your OG will be in the 1.030 to 1.034 range, although this will depend on how much sugar remained in your fermented kombucha. You may add more sugar at this time if you would like a higher starting gravity. I do not

recommend going over 1.040 when you are beginning boozy buch brewing.

6. Add the rehydrated yeast solution.

7. Seal your jar with a grommeted lid or stopper and filled airlock.

8. Use the SCOBY and reserved kombucha to begin a new batch of kombucha, using the directions for primary kombucha fermentation on page 127.

9. Ferment your boozy buch between 68°F and 80°F for 7 to 14 days, until desired taste is obtained.

10. Bottle as directed on pages 26 to 31.

Variations

- **Flavored Rooibos Tea:** Rooibos teas work beautifully in boozy buches and come in a wide variety of flavors. Start with 2 tea bags and adjust as desired.

- **Ginger Pear White Tea:** Substitute 3 ginger pear white tea bags for the spearmint tea.

- **Pomegranate White Tea:** Use 2 pomegranate white tea bags in place of the spearmint tea.

- **Coconut Green Tea with Lemongrass and Ginger:** Use 4 grams of loose coconut green tea with lemongrass and ginger in place of the spearmint tea. This is especially lovely with a jun culture.

133

RHUBARB KEFIR BEER

Rhubarb is the perfect complement to kefir beer. This is a delicious sweet-tart fruity beverage that is the perfect shade of rose. I stock up on rhubarb during the season, then blanch and freeze it for use throughout the year. **Yield: *1 gallon***

- **1 gal. fermented water kefir (see page 128)**
- **½ cup sugar**
- **¾ cup diced fresh or frozen rhubarb**
- **½ packet champagne yeast**
- **1 tsp. Go-Ferm (approximately 3 g)**
- **¹/₁₆ tsp beer yeast nutrient**

Instructions

1. Hydrate the yeast with Go-Ferm. Heat ¼ cup water to 104°F. Stir in 1 teaspoon of Go-Ferm and sprinkle ½ packet of champagne yeast on top. Let stand for 20 minutes.

2. Heat ½ cup water to a boil. Place the rhubarb and ½ cup sugar in a heat-resistant pitcher or saucepan. Pour the off-boil water over the rhubarb and sugar and stir until sugar is dissolved.

3. Strain the fermented water kefir into the jar, capturing the grains in the mesh strainer. Set the strainer to the side over a clean surface (a mug or glass pitcher works well).

4. Add a dash of beer yeast nutrient and stir gently to combine.

5. You may take a gravity reading using your hydrometer or refractometer at this point if you choose. Your OG will be in the 1.030 to 1.034 range, although this will depend on how much sugar remained in your fermented water kefir. You may add more sugar at this time if you would like a higher starting gravity. I do not recommend going over 1.040 when you are beginning kefir beer brewing.

6. Add the rehydrated yeast solution.

7. Seal the jar with a grommeted lid or stopper and filled airlock.

8. Use the reserved grains to begin a new batch of water kefir, using the directions for primary water kefir fermentation on page 128.

9. Ferment between 68°F and 80°F for 7 to 14 days, until desired taste is obtained.

10. Bottle as instructed on pages 26 to 31.

Variations

- **Strawberry Water Kefir:** Skip step
  number 2 and use 1 cup whole fresh or
  frozen strawberries instead of rhubarb.
  Wash and thaw your strawberries before
  using. You may remove the green leafy
  tops, but I do not find this necessary.

135

STRAWBERRY-SAAZ KEFIR BEER

Hops make the perfect addition to kefir beer; their unique aromas and flavors really shine in this beverage, and the bitterness adds balance. I love using single varieties of hops with complementary fruit flavoring. Strawberry-Saaz and Mango-Citra are two of my favorites, but a wide variety of aromatic hops are available. The amount of hops to use is extremely variable; I tend to prefer a less bitter beverage, but many of my testers preferred the more bitter version. It's very personal, so feel free to adjust up or down the amount of hops that you add. **Yield: *1 gallon***

- **1 gal. fermented water kefir (see page 128)**
- **½ c. sugar**
- **15 medium strawberries, washed, with green tops removed**
- **0.5 oz. Saaz hop pellets (for a less bitter beverage, use 0.25 oz.)**
- **½ packet of champagne yeast**
- **1 tsp. Go-Ferm (approximately 3 g)**
- **1/16 tsp beer yeast nutrient**

Instructions

1. Hydrate the yeast with Go-Ferm. Heat ¼ cup water to 104°F. Stir in 1 teaspoon of Go-Ferm and sprinkle ½ packet of champagne yeast on top. Let stand for 20 minutes.

2. Add the strawberries and hops to a sanitized 1-gallon wide-mouth jar.

3. Strain the fermented water kefir into the jar, capturing the grains in the mesh strainer. Set the strainer to the side over a clean surface. (A mug or glass pitcher works well.)

4. Add a dash of beer yeast nutrient and stir gently to combine.

5. You may take a gravity reading using your hydrometer or refractometer at this point if you choose. Your OG will be in the 1.030 to 1.034 range, although this will depend on how much sugar remained in your fermented water kefir. You may add more sugar at this time if you would like a higher starting gravity. I do not recommend going over 1.040 when you are beginning kefir beer brewing.

BITTERNESS WITHOUT HEAT?

As explained on page 47, alpha acids are the primary compound in hops responsible for bitterness in beer. However, alpha acids are relatively insoluble in water-based solutions and must be isomerized into iso-alpha acids in order to provide bitterness in beer. (Isomerization is simply a change in the structure of a molecule without altering the formula.) While boiling is the most common way for brewers to isomerize alpha acids, other methods may accomplish the process as well, including chemical extraction. Water kefir contains a myriad of compounds due in part to the diversity of the fermenting culture. While I have not come across a study that explains the exact bittering contribution of hops in kefir beer, I have firsthand experience and can tell you the addition of hop pellets adds not only aroma and flavor but also bitterness, leaving me to assume that one of the compounds produced as a byproduct of fermentation is isomerizing the alpha acids.

6. Add the rehydrated yeast solution.

7. Seal the jar with a grommeted lid or stopper and filled airlock.

8. Use the reserved grains to begin a new batch of water kefir, using the directions for primary water kefir fermentation on page 128.

9. Ferment between 68°F and 80°F for 7 to 14 days, until desired taste is obtained.

10. Bottle as instructed on pages 26 to 31.

Variations

- **Mango-Citra Kefir Beer:** Substitute 1 ounce freeze-dried mango and 0.4 oz of Citra hop pellets for the strawberries and Saaz hops.

- **For a nonbitter hopped water kefir,** add your hop pellets at the end of fermentation and hold at refrigerator temperature for 24 to 48 hours before straining and packaging, similar to the Dry-Hopped Cider method on page 107.

DEVELOPING YOUR OWN
BOOZY BUCH & KEFIR BEER

THE TANGY ACETIC NOTES of boozy buch play wonderfully with so many flavors. You can accentuate the tartness by adding like flavors, such as lemon, lime, or hibiscus. Or add some contrast with earthier herbs and spices, such as allspice or ginger. Browse the tea section of your local grocery store or, better yet, seek out a specialty tea store. You will be amazed and tempted by the selection—and almost any herbal, flavored, or specialty tea blend will work as a flavoring when you're turning your regular kombucha into a batch of boozy buch. Of course, you can always combine fruits with teas; there's a wonderful world of flavors out there that are practically begging to be made into a boozy buch.

While kefir beer is similar, I tend to approach flavoring it a bit differently. It can ferment out quite clean yet with more residual body than many of the spirited sodas in the next chapter. Kefir beer displays hops so beautifully that I am continuing to play with all kinds of hop and fruit combinations. And kefir beer works perfectly for all of the natural soda recipes that are out there.

Boozy buch and kefir beer are relatively new and unknown beverages, yet they are incredibly delicious and have so much potential to showcase a world of flavors. Snag yourself a SCOBY or batch of kefir grains and enjoy exploring the world of mixed-culture alcoholic fermentations!

6

///////////

SPIRITED SODA

LIKE MOST BREWERS, I was skeptical about sugar-based fermented beverages before I made one. Barley, apple juice, and honey are all less refined and have more personality than plain sugar. But coming across a recipe for spinach wine in an English World War II–era cookbook was the shot in the arm that I needed. It just sounded too weird not to try. So I whipped up a one-gallon batch, and it was seriously tasty! As I kept seeing sugar-based fermented beverages in my research of alcoholic beverages around the world, I came to accept the facts: humans have been using various forms of sugar to feed yeast for a very long time, and people have enjoyed the results.

To me, a spirited soda is a delicious fermented drink that showcases the beauty of the ingredients it was made from. By that I mean: when designing beer, cider, and short mead recipes, I think about the barley, apple juice, and honey as the stars of the show and any flavorings as the supporting cast. But for spirited sodas, I want the specialty ingredients to take the lead. With that in mind, I decided to split this chapter into two parts: Fruity and Floral Spirited Sodas and Herb, Spice, and Root Spirited Sodas. The Fruity and Floral Spirited Sodas are just that: they contain fruit, fruit juice, or floral water in addition to sugar. The Herb, Spice, and Root Spirited Sodas are a bit different. Although they contain a variety of herbs, spices, and roots, they utilize crystal malt in addition to the sugar. They take a bit longer to prepare than the fruity and floral sodas, but significantly less than a traditional beer.

FRUITY & FLORAL SPIRITED SODA

THERE REALLY AREN'T any commercially produced beverages that correlate to what you'll brew in this chapter. Yet it's hard to taste them and not try to compare them to something else that you drink on a regular basis. It's kind of like when people taste a new kind of meat, whether it be armadillo or alligator or antelope. "Tastes like chicken" is an inevitable response. We're always seeking to liken new flavors to something that we're comfortable with. While these beverages are akin to ciders and beers and the like, they just don't fit those categories exactly. And that's a good thing. As the saying goes, variety is the spice of life. Think about these beverages as you would a new cuisine, with an open mind and hearty appetite. I think you'll be very pleased with the results.

INGREDIENTS

Fruit Juices, Nectars, and Syrups

Almost any fruit or fruit combination may be used for these recipes. The only rule for choosing a fruit juice, nectar, or syrup is to avoid ones with added preservatives. Juices with sorbates, benzoates, or sulfites are not suitable for fermenting. Juices containing citric acid, malic acid, ascorbic acid, or lemon juice may be used, though results may vary. Either 100 percent juice or juice with sugar added is the best choice.

Containers labeled as juice typically contain 100 percent fruit juice, while a nectar has sugar and/or preservatives added. A syrup is a concentrated juice, often with sugar added.

I find the best juices for fermenting in international groceries or in the international aisles of grocery stores. I use a lot of juices, nectars, and syrups from Mexico, Latin America, and Eastern and Central Europe in my fermented beverages. They come in a wide range of fruits and are often

100 percent juice or have acceptable additives, like sugar and lemon juice. They're also usually priced much more economically than fruit juices from gourmet or health food stores, which are also good sources for suitable fruit juices. When using a new fruit juice, nectar or syrup, take the gravity of the liquid first. If the gravity is lower than your target original gravity, you will need to add sugar. If it's higher, you will need to dilute it with water.

You can also make your own fresh fruit juice if you own a juicer. Begin with the freshest, ripest, and sweetest fruit that you can find. I always wash my fruit and usually sanitize it if I am not removing the peel or rind. If you don't have a juicer, you can use a blender or food processor to puree fruits then strain the puree through several layers of cheesecloth. This is more time-consuming than using a juicer but does work for softer fruits, such as watermelon.

Herbs and Spices

Both fresh and dried herbs and spices may be used, although each form contributes a slightly different character to the finished beverage. Fresher is better, regardless of whether they're fresh or dried. The aromatic and flavor compounds are more concentrated in dried herbs and spices, so you will need to use a smaller quantity of them than you would if using fresh herbs and spices. If you're using dried herbs or spices, steep them in off-boil water for five to fifteen minutes, depending on the freshness of the herb or spice and the flavor desired. Fresh herbs can be treated the same way, or they can be sanitized and added directly to the fermentation vessel.

Fruit

Choose the highest-quality fruit that you can find. The riper, fresher, and sweeter the fruit, the better your end beverage will taste. I wash my fruit and sanitize it if I am using the zest or peel in a recipe. Freeze-dried fruit may also be used.

Sugar

A variety of sugars may be used in spirited sodas. I recommend organic white sugar in the majority of the recipes, as it provides a clean background for the flavors. Less-refined sugars may be used; they may add more aroma and flavor character to the finished beverage. Refer to the master sugar list on pages 13 to 16.

Yeast

I've found that there isn't much difference in the aroma, flavor, or body of the spirited soda between using champagne yeast, American ale yeast, or English ale yeast in the majority of these recipes. I prefer dry champagne yeast as it easy to divide, works fast, and has a wider temperature and pH tolerance, but I've made most of these with liquid ale yeast as well. Choose champagne yeast if speed is your priority; choose ale yeast if you'd like a more leisurely ferment. Champagne yeast can chew through these beverages pretty quickly, so ale yeast can give you a bit more of a cushion if you find that your spirited sodas are fermenting too fast and becoming drier than you like.

Water

Filtered, chlorine-free water is best.

HOW to MAKE FRUITY & FLORAL SPIRITED SODA

The following equipment and instructions are scaled for a 1-gallon batch size.

Materials

- 1-gallon jug or wide-mouth jar
- Cleanser and sanitizer
- Stopper or grommeted lid and airlock
- Stainless-steel spoon (if stirring is required)
- Plastic mesh strainer and funnel
- Hydrometer
- Recipe and ingredients
- Brewing notebook

Instructions

1. Clean and sanitize all equipment, including the 1-gallon jug or wide-mouth jar that will be used as the fermentation vessel.

2. If using dried herbs or spices, first make a tea by steeping herbs and spices in off-boil water for 10 to 15 minutes.

3. Add juice, flavorings, and/or tea to the 1-gallon jug or wide-mouth jar.

4. Add sugar, top with filtered water to reach 1 gallon, and stir with a sanitized spoon or cap and shake to thoroughly combine.

5. Take a gravity reading, if desired.

6. Pitch yeast and ferment at 65°F to 70°F for 5 to 10 days.

GUAVA SODA

Guava is such a lovely, complex fruit; it's perfect for a fermented soda. I was thrilled when I came across a preservative-free guava nectar in the international aisle of my local grocery store, but I wasn't sure how it would ferment out. Turns out I had nothing to worry about; the aroma and flavor of the guava carry through beautifully. This is fruity, floral, and a bit perfumelike, yet highly drinkable. I've fermented a variety of juices, nectars, and syrups, but this is hands-down my favorite. **Yield: *1 gallon***

- ¾ gal. filtered water
- 1 L preservative-free guava nectar
- 250 g sugar (preferably white, but any combination of sugars may be used)
- ½ pack English ale yeast
- 1/16 tsp. beer yeast nutrient

Instructions

1. Add guava nectar to a sanitized 1-gallon jug or jar.
2. Add sugar and beer yeast nutrient and top off with filtered water to reach 1 gallon.
3. Cap or stopper and shake to dissolve sugar and beer yeast nutrient.
4. You may take a gravity reading using a hydrometer or refractometer at this point if you choose. The OG should be in the 1.040 to 1.044 range.
5. Pitch ½ packet of English ale yeast and top with a grommeted lid or stopper and filled airlock.
6. Ferment for 4 to 7 days at 66°F to 72°F.
7. Bottle as instructed on pages 26 to 31.

Variations

- **Hopped Guava Soda:** Hop your soda by adding pellet hops 2 to 3 days before you bottle. Strain hop pellets out when you bottle.
- **Herbed or Spiced Soda:** For dried or woody herbs and spices, make a tea by steeping your spices for 10 minutes in off-boil water. Fresh, fleshy herbs and spices may be added directly to your base liquid or be infused into a tea first.

ROSE CARDAMOM SODA

This recipe is inspired by one of my favorite desserts, kheer, a South Asian rice pudding flavored with cardamom and rose water. These complex flavors shine in a clean fermented soda base. This is one of my favorite fermented dessert beverages after a spicy Indian meal. **Yield: *1 gallon***

- 1 gal. filtered, chlorine-free water
- 1½ c. white sugar
- ¼ c. of rose water (available at Middle Eastern groceries)
- 3 green cardamom pods, cracked
- ½ packet champagne yeast
- 1/16 tsp. beer yeast nutrient

Instructions

1. Bring ½ cup of filtered, chlorine-free water to a boil.
2. Pour the ½ cup of off-boil water over the cardamom pods and steep for 10 minutes.
3. After 10 minutes, dissolve the 1½ cups of sugar into the cardamom tea and stir to combine.
4. Add the ¼ cup rose water and yeast nutrient to a sanitized 1-gallon jug or jar.
5. Pour the sweetened cardamom tea into the sanitized wide-mouth jar, straining out the cardamom pods.
6. Top off with chlorine-free water to 1 gallon and stir to combine.
7. You may take a gravity reading using a hydrometer or refractometer at this point if you choose. The OG should be in the 1.030 to 1.034 range.
8. Pitch ½ packet of champagne yeast and top with a grommeted lid or stopper and filled airlock.
9. Ferment 5 to 9 days at 65°F to 70°F.
10. Bottle as instructed on page 26 to 31.

Variations

- **Orange Blossom–Anise Soda:**
Take a cue from Moroccan
desserts and replace the rose
water with the same amount of
orange blossom water and the
cardamom pods with ½ teaspoon
of anise seed.

- **Orange Blossom–Cinnamon
Soda:** This is another popular
combination in Moroccan
desserts. Replace the rose water
with the same amount of orange
blossom water and the cardamom
pods with ½ stick of cinnamon.

- **Use English ale yeast** for a
fruitier soda or saison yeast
for a fruitier, more floral soda.

- **Increase or decrease** the
amount of rose water. I love this
soda with ½ cup of rose water.

- **Replace the sugar** with 1
pound 4 ounces of honey to make
a rose-cardamom short mead.

SPIRITED SODA

RHUBARB SODA

Ah, spring. Here in New York City, the city comes back to life—the dirty gray slush melts, flowers bloom in tree pits, and the Green Markets pop with color: strawberries, fresh greens, and my favorite, rhubarb. Rhubarb season is short, so I buy as many of these tart fuchsia stalks as I can. I dice them, blanch them, and freeze them for use year round in desserts—and, of course, in fermented beverages. Rhubarb can add flavor to many beverages, but my favorite is rhubarb soda; it's tart, fruity, and delicious. This is spring in a glass. **Yield: *1 gallon***

- **1 gal. filtered, chlorine-free water**
- **1½ c. white sugar**
- **1 lb. 8 oz. cleaned and diced rhubarb**
- **½ packet champagne yeast**
- **1/16 tsp. beer yeast nutrient**

Instructions

1. Mix diced rhubarb and sugar in a heat-resistant bowl. Cover bowl and macerate for 8 to 12 hours.*
2. Bring 2 cups of water to a boil.
3. Uncover the rhubarb-sugar mixture and add beer yeast nutrient.
4. Pour the 2 cups of off-boil water over the rhubarb-sugar-nutrient mixture. Immediately chill in an ice bath or by adding sanitary filtered ice cubes.
5. Pour the rhubarb mixture into a sanitized wide-mouth jar. (Do not strain the rhubarb out.)
6. Top off with chlorine-free water to 1 gallon and stir to combine.
7. You may take a gravity reading using a hydrometer or refractometer at this point if you choose. The OG should be in the 1.030 to 1.034 range.
8. Pitch ½ packet of champagne yeast and top with a grommeted lid and filled airlock.
9. Ferment 5 to 9 days at 65°F to 70°F.
10. Bottle as instructed on page 26 to 31.

*Maceration is the process of softening fresh produce in liquid or sugar. This process draws out the juices, making the produce softer and more flavorful. Fibrous fruits, vegetables, and herbs often benefit from maceration before being cooked with or fermented.

Variations

- **Strawberry-Rhubarb Soda:** Add ½ cup of freeze-dried strawberries or a cup of fresh strawberries, tops removed and sliced, when you add the beer yeast nutrient.
- **Use English ale yeast** for a fruitier soda or saison yeast for a fruitier, more floral soda.
- **Other fruits may be used.** I like to freeze fresh fruit, thaw, and muddle slightly before using in a soda.

WATERMELON MINT SODA

Watermelon is an elusive aroma and flavor to capture. Watermelon candies and watermelon beers are often artificial in character. My friend Keith makes a spectacular watermelon beer, but he uses an outrageous amount of fruit in each batch, making it both impractical and costly to brew. And for every one of his delicious watermelon ales, I've had at least three unsavory watermelon beers—either too sweet and/or with an artificial watermelon character. But watermelon can shine in the right environment, and this Watermelon Mint Soda is it. The fermented soda is never better than the juice it begins with, so start with a good, ripe watermelon—the sweeter the better. The mint and lime complement the sweetness of the watermelon. **Yield: *1 gallon***

- 1 gal. filtered, chlorine-free water
- 1½ c. white sugar
- 6 oz. agave nectar
- 2 c. fresh watermelon juice (use a juicer or a blender and a strainer to obtain fresh juice)
- 5 fresh mint leaves, muddled
- ⅛ tsp. freshly grated lime zest
- ½ tsp. fresh-squeezed lime juice
- ½ packet English ale yeast (wet or dry)
- ¹⁄₁₆ tsp. beer yeast nutrient

Instructions

1. Bring 2 cups of water to a boil. Add agave nectar, sugar, and yeast nutrient to a heat-resistant pitcher.
2. Pour off-boil water into the pitcher and stir to dissolve.
3. Cool sugar mixture to below 75°F, either in an ice bath or by adding sanitary ice cubes.
4. Add watermelon juice, mint, lime zest, and juice to a sanitized 1-gallon jug or jar.
5. Add cooled sugar mixture to the jug or jar, top with enough filtered water to reach 1 gallon, and stir or shake to combine.
6. You may take a gravity reading using a hydrometer or refractometer at this point if you choose. The OG should be in the 1.046 to 1.050 range.
7. Pitch ½ packet of yeast and top with a grommeted lid or stopper and filled airlock.
8. Ferment 12 to 14 days at 65°F to 70°F.
9. Bottle as instructed on page s 26 to 31.

HERB, SPICE & ROOT SPIRITED SODA

LOVE OLD-FASHIONED SODAS—the nonalcoholic ones made from scratch with bark, herbs, spices, and sugar. I've made several, and I'm lucky that my favorite local bar offers two house-made herbal sodas, a root beer and a cola. I've had some lovely root beer meads, sarsaparilla beers, and the like. But I wanted to ferment a drink in which the roots, spices, and herbs of traditional sodas were the main focus. So I tried fermenting one of my old standard soda recipes as is. Unfortunately, the sugar completely fermented out, leaving me with a thin, bitter boozy beverage with no residual sweetness whatsoever. It was a great mixer, but a no-go for a spirited soda. So I tried adding steeped crystal malts, which leave some residual sugar in the mix. Success! You can also use these recipes to make an unfermented nonalcoholic traditional soda if you have access to kegging equipment. Scale the flavorings up for your batch size, omit the crystal malt, add sugar to taste, cool, keg, and force-carbonate.

INGREDIENTS

Crystal Malt
Crystal malt is barley malt that has essentially been stewed during the kilning process, meaning that the starches have been converted to sugars in the kernel. Some of those sugars aren't fully fermentable, so they leave some residual sweetness and add body to the finished beverage. Crystal malts need to be crushed and steeped between 150°F and 170°F to release the sugars contained inside the kernel. Crystal malts also contribute color, aroma, and flavor to your finished drink.

Sugar
White sugar will provide a neutral background for your herbal sodas, while less refined sugar may contribute some aroma and flavor character. Refer to the master sugar list on pages 13 to 16.

Herbs and Spices

I used dried herbs and spices for the majority of my herbal and spiced sodas. Use the freshest dried herbs and spices that you can find. Although many of the herbs and spices may be found in your spice cabinet, a few are less common. These may be ordered from specialty purveyors online or found in health food stores, international groceries, and herb and spice specialty stores. I order the harder-to-find herbs and spices that I use most frequently in bulk online and purchase the rest by the ounce at local specialty stores.

Yeast

Dry or wet yeast may be used for these sodas. Dry champagne yeast and wet or dry English or American ale yeasts gave me the best results. I recommend champagne yeast if you prefer a drier soda and American or English ale yeast if you prefer a less dry soda.

HOW to MAKE HERB, SPICE & ROOT SPIRITED SODA

The following equipment and instructions are scaled for a one-gallon batch size.

Materials
- Basic Brewing Equipment (pages 17–24)
- 1-gallon jug or wide-mouth jar
- 1–2 gallon stainless-steel pot
- Cleanser and sanitizer
- Brew bag
- Stainless-steel spoon
- Thermometer
- Hydrometer
- Packaging equipment (for kegging or bottling)
- Recipe and ingredients
- 1 gallon filtered water

Instructions
1. Fill the pot with 10 cups of water.
2. Preheat your oven to the lowest setting. You want it to be somewhere in the 150°F to 175°F range.
3. Bring the water in the pot to a temperature between 156°F and 168°F.
4. Once the water is at strike temperature, turn off the heat and insert the brew bag. Add the crushed grain, stirring to avoid dough balls. Adding the grain and

stirring should bring the temperature down to between 150°F and 166°F. Close your grain bag and secure with a loose knot or twist.

5. Turn off the oven, place the lid on your pot, and place the pot in the preheated oven. Set your timer for 30 minutes.

6. While the grains are steeping, fill your clean jug or wide-mouth jar with sanitizing solution. Fill a second container (large enough to fit the thermometer, stainless-steel spoon, lid or stopper, airlock, strainer, and yeast packet) with sanitizing solution. Place those items into solution.

7. After 20 minutes has passed, heat 2 cups of water in a saucepan or teakettle. Once water reaches a boil, pour over your herbs and spice mixture in a heat-resistant container.

8. After 30 minutes has passed, remove the brew kettle and place it back on the burner. Remove the grain bag and squeeze gently to drain.

9. Bring the wort to a boil. Once the wort comes to a boil, add your sugars and beer yeast nutrient, stirring to combine

ingredients and to prevent sugar from scorching and.

10. Boil wort for 10 minutes.

11. Remove from heat and add flavoring tea, straining out herbs and spices.

12. Chill wort in an ice bath to just below 70°F.

13. Empty the fermentation vessel of sanitizing solution and transfer the wort from the pot to the vessel by pouring it through a sanitized plastic funnel and strainer.

14. Add filtered water to reach 1 gallon. Stir to combine.

15. Remove a sample large enough to take a gravity reading.

16. Pitch the yeast, place the lid or stopper and airlock on the fermentation vessel, and let the magic happen. Remember to monitor the temperature of your fermentation and keep it in the appropriate range for the yeast.

Note: Fermentation temperature control is very important in the first few days of the ferment. Maintain as steady a temperature as possible while fermenting your spirited soda.

ABSINTHOLA

I went through an absinthe obsession several years ago. Friends of mine had tucked a bottle into their luggage on a trip back from Europe. They served it after a dinner party at their apartment, and I was smitten. This was before absinthe was re-legalized in the United States, and alas, I was unable to procure a bottle of my own. So I did the next best thing: I researched the flavoring ingredients and started making Absinthola. This was an unfermented soda; I steeped up the herbs and spices, added sugar, kegged and carbonated it, and kept it on draft. It was lovely and a hit at parties, with or without the added vodka. When I began planning the recipes for this chapter, Absinthola was the first to come to mind. So here is my original Absinthola recipe brewed with Crystal 20—not quite a beer but dangerously drinkable and a bit exotic to boot. **Yield: *1 gallon***

- **1 gal. filtered, chlorine-free water**
- **1 lb. Crystal 20 malt, crushed**
- **1½ c. white sugar**
- **1 tbsp. star anise**
- **1 tbsp. fennel**
- **1 tsp. licorice root**
- **1 tsp. lemon balm**
- **1 tsp. hyssop**
- **1 tsp. calamus**
- **1 tsp. wormwood**
- **½ packet dry champagne yeast**
- **1/16 tsp. beer yeast nutrient**

Instructions

For complete brewing instructions, see pages 156–157.

1. Heat 10 cups of water to 156°F to 168°F and add the bag of crushed malt. The steeping temperature should be 150°F to 166°F after adding the grain bag. Place in an oven and steep for 30 minutes.

2. After malt has been steeping for 20 minutes, heat 2 cups of water. Once water is boiling, pour over dried herbs and spices to steep.

3. After malt has steeped for 30 minutes, place the pot back on the stove, remove grain bag, and gently squeeze to drain.

4. Bring the wort to a boil. Once the boil is rolling, stir in the beer yeast nutrient and sugar, stirring to avoid scorching and mix thoroughly.

5. Boil for 10 minutes.

6. Remove from heat and add the tea, straining out the herbs and spices.

7. Chill in an ice bath to just below 70°F.

8. Transfer to a sanitized fermentation vessel, add filtered water to top off to 1 gallon, and stir to combine.

9. Remove a sample to take a gravity reading, if desired. The gravity should be 1.042 to 1.044.

10. Pitch the yeast.

11. Ferment at 65°F to 70°F. The fermentation should finish in 5 to 10 days. To bottle, follow master directions on pages 26 to 31.

SPIRITED SODA

GIN-OLA

I love the complexity of a good gin but don't always want the booze that goes with it. So I created this fermented soda using the herbs and spices that give gin its distinctive aroma and flavor. Use champagne yeast for a drier version and English ale yeast for a soda with slightly more residual sugar. Just as there are many different gins, there can be many different versions of this soda. I encourage you to use this recipe as a jumping-off point; feel free to play with both the ratios and the types of herbs and spices used. **Yield: *1 gallon***

- **1 gal. filtered, chlorine-free water**
- **1 lb. Crystal 20 malt, crushed**
- **1½ c. white sugar**
- **1 tbsp. juniper berries**
- **¼ tsp. coriander**
- **1 tsp. chamomile**
- **½ tsp. lavender**
- **2 green cardamom pods, cracked**
- **½ bay leaf**
- **2 allspice berries**
- **4-in. slice grapefruit peel (zest only, no pith)**
- **½ packet champagne yeast or English ale yeast**
- **¹⁄₁₆ tsp. beer yeast nutrient**

Instructions

For complete brewing instructions, see pages 156–157.

1. Heat 10 cups of water to 156°F to 168°F and add the bag of crushed crystal malt. Add the juniper berries directly to the water. The steeping temperature should be 150°F to 166°F. Place in an oven and steep for 30 minutes.

2. After malt has been steeping for 20 minutes, heat 2 cups of water. Once water is boiling, pour over remaining dried herbs and spices to steep.

3. After malt has steeped for 30 minutes, place the pot back on the stove, remove grain bag, and gently squeeze to drain.

4. Bring the wort to a boil. Once the boil is rolling, stir in the beer yeast nutrient and sugar, stirring to avoid scorching, and mix thoroughly.

5. Boil for 10 minutes.

6. Remove from heat and add the tea, straining out the herbs and spices.

7. Chill in an ice bath to just below 70°F.

8. Transfer to a sanitized fermentation vessel, straining out the juniper berries. Add filtered water to top off to 1 gallon and stir to combine.

9. Remove a sample to take a gravity reading, if desired. The gravity should be 1.042 to 1.044.

10. Pitch the yeast.

11. Ferment at 65°F to 70°F. The fermentation should finish in 5 to 10 days. To bottle, follow master directions on pages 26 to 31.

SALTED LICORICE SODA

Salted licorice gummy fish from Germany are among my favorite candies of all time. The saltiness complements the chewy rich sweetness perfectly. **Yield: *1 gallon***

- 1 gal. filtered, chlorine-free water
- 1 lb. Crystal 80 malt, crushed
- 1½ c. panela (or other brown sugar)
- ½ tbsp. molasses
- 1 tbsp. licorice root
- ½ tsp. anise seed
- 1 star anise pod
- ⅛ tsp. salt
- ½ packet champagne yeast or English ale yeast
- 1/16 tsp. beer yeast nutrient

Instructions

For complete brewing instructions, see pages 156–157.

1. Heat 10 cups of water to 156°F to 168°F and add the bag of crushed crystal malt. The steeping temperature should be 150°F to 166°F. Place in an oven and steep for 30 minutes.
2. After malt has been steeping for 20 minutes, heat 2 cups of water. Once water is boiling, pour over dried spices to steep.
3. After malt has steeped for 30 minutes, place the pot back on the stove, remove grain bag, and gently squeeze to drain.
4. Bring the wort to a boil. Once the boil is rolling, stir in the beer yeast nutrient, sugar, and molasses, stirring to avoid scorching and mix thoroughly.
5. Boil for 10 minutes.
6. Remove from heat and add the salt and the tea, straining out the herbs and spices.
7. Chill in an ice bath to just below 70°F.
8. Transfer to a sanitized fermentation vessel. Add filtered water to top off to 1 gallon and stir to combine.
9. Remove a sample to take a gravity reading, if desired. The gravity should be 1.032 to 1.036.
10. Pitch the yeast.
11. Ferment at 65°F to 70°F. The fermentation should finish in 5 to 10 days. To bottle, follow master directions on pages 26 to 31.

DEVELOPING YOUR OWN SPIRITED SODA

SPIRITED SODAS are probably the most open type of fermented beverages to brew. When I get a flavor-driven idea for a new fermented beverage, I run through the spectrum of sugar sources to use. Are those flavors best showcased in a cider, mead, boozy buch, or beer? Or perhaps they need a sugar base to really shine? If sugar is where I land, I focus on the type of sugar and yeast and the amounts and ratios of the flavoring ingredients. Often I'll make a couple of half-gallon test batches, using different amounts of flavorings or types of sugar. Or I'll make a gallon and split it into two half-gallon batches, using two different yeasts. If the flavorings are purely root and spice-based, I'll choose a crystal malt soda and make several test batches using different types of crystal malts and yeasts. You can often get these right on the first go, but small test batches of these beverages are really fun and will help you drill down to the perfect spirited soda. Otherwise, I cruise my local international groceries for interesting preservative-free juices, the Green Market for fresh local produce, and spice stores for interesting and unusual spices. There is a whole world of flavors out there that is begging to be captured and fermented into a spirited soda. Pick up something new and ferment it into something intoxicatingly wonderful!

7

//////////////////

FAR-FLUNG FERMENTS

WHILE MANY MODERN-DAY BREWERS painstakingly brew their beverages using specialty ingredients, the strictest sanitary practices, and state-of-the-art equipment, spontaneously fast-fermented beverages still have a place in households around the world.

I stumbled upon one these beverages on a recent trip to Cambodia, when I stopped off at a roadside palm sugar stand. Our guide explained that the men harvest palm sap from local palm trees, and the women cook it into palm sugar over wood fires. As we tasted fresh-cooked palm sugar, I recalled reading about a fermented palm sap beverage, and I asked if the families made beverages from the sap as well. One of the women ducked into a nearby house and a few minutes later, out came her husband with a tin cup and a plastic water bottle full of a milky white liquid. As we shared this delightful, refreshing, and slightly funky drink, we asked about the process. Translation was a bit rough, but the lowdown was that the men climb a palm tree (using a rather frightening makeshift ladder consisting of a sapling tree lashed to the palm trunk), collect the sap in a plastic bucket, add local roots, and leave it out for a couple of days to ferment. We brought the remainder of the bottle back to our hotel, placed it in the fridge overnight, and drank the rest the next day. It was even better—smoother and very carbonated, showing that this was still actively fermenting. Although I had read about these types of beverages, this was a real eye-opener and inspiration to me.

FERMENTED BEVERAGES AROUND THE WORLD

MOST INDIGENOUS FERMENTED BEVERAGES utilize whatever ingredients are readily available and abundant, from locally grown produce and grains to tree sap to foraged bark and roots. The majority of these beverages are fermented openly and spontaneously, using yeasts and bacteria endemic to the area. For this chapter, I've adapted several traditionally fermented beverages to utilize ingredients readily available in the United States. I also recommend using commercial yeast, as it provides a much more predictable result in aroma and flavor as well as in alcohol levels than your local yeast and bacteria strains do. That said, I encourage you to experiment with both local ingredients and local yeasts and bacteria. For example, if you're in New England and have maple trees on your property, fresh maple sap is a sugar solution begging to be converted to alcohol. Or perhaps you're in the Southwest and have a prickly pear cactus in your yard? That's fair game, too. Bottom line: you can ferment almost anything, as long as it has sugar in it.

The recipes in this chapter use a variety of techniques, many of which have been explained in previous chapters. We'll be creating some kind of sugar-laden substrate for the yeast to feed on and produce alcohol and carbon dioxide.

Burukutu

Burukutu is a fermented sorghum drink from Nigeria. Sorghum is germinated, sun-dried, and brewed similar to barley-based beer. A previous batch of burukutu or commercial yeast is used to ferment the beverage over a couple of days. The drink is then boiled and matured for an additional couple of days. Other cereal-based beverages are brewed throughout Africa using maize, millet, and rice, depending what is available. These beverages are low in alcohol and typically sour from *Lactobacillus* or *Acetobacter* fermentation.

Chicha

Chicha is a fermented maize-based beverage made in Central and South American countries. Traditional Chicha de Muko is created by grinding dried maize, moistening it in the mouth with saliva, forming it into cakes and naturally fermenting. Our spit contains enzymes that help convert the corn starches and this traditional step takes the place of malting. Alternatively, chicha de jora is a version that uses a more modern method of germination and malting to prepare the corn for brewing. Fermented versions are finished in a couple of days and are usually below 4 percent in alcohol content, and nonfermented versions also exist. A variety of other grains and starches such as quinoa, cassava, plantain, and amaranth may be used instead of or in addition to the corn. Fruits, herbs, and spices such as strawberries, cinnamon, pineapple, lime, coriander, and coca leaf may be added for flavoring.

Kvass

Kvass is a fermented beverage made from bread in Russia, Ukraine, Latvia, and other Eastern European countries. Kvass is fermented naturally or with a cultured starter, similar to those used for sourdough breads. It is typically below 3 percent ABV and may be flavored with mint or fruit. Beet kvass is a nonalcoholic version that is lacto-fermented, with whey or another culture that contains *Lactobacillus*. (For a recipe, see page 180.)

Makgeolli

Makgeolli is a fermented Korean rice beverage also known as makkoli or makuly. To make makgeolli, sweet rice is cooked, cooled, mixed with water, and inoculated with a dried mixed culture that contains *Aspergillus*, *Rhizopus*, and yeasts. Makgeolli is allowed to ferment for around four days and can contain up to 8 percent ABV. It is cloudy white and slightly sour.

Mauby

Mauby is a sugar-based spiced beverage popular in the Caribbean. Nonfermented and fermented versions exist. Mauby bark, a slightly bitter bark from the buckthorn shrub, is the base flavoring, and a variety of spices and herbs are used in addition. Mauby is naturally fermented or fermented using a starter culture from a previous batch. (For a recipe, see page 174.)

Mbege

Mbege is a fermented banana beverage native to Tanzania. It's also known as urwaga in Kenya, as lubisi in Uganda, and as urwagwa in Rwanda. Bananas are ripened, mashed, and cooked, and millet or sorghum is often added to stimulate fermentation. (See Berliner Weisse technique on page 68.). Fermentation lasts for around twenty-four hours before the beverage is filtered and consumed.

Oskola

Fresh birch sap is fermented for this refreshing beverage, which is a light, low-alcohol, spontaneously fermented drink found in Poland, Latvia, and other countries where birch trees thrive. I've had a couple of beers made with fresh maple and birch sap, and I encourage you to play around with this raw sugar source if you live in an area where it is produced. Fresh sap has a short shelf life and must be processed in a timely manner.

Pulque

Pulque is made by fermenting fresh agave sap. It is served at pulquerías in Mexico and is sometimes flavored with fresh fruit pulp. (For recipes, see pages 182 and 184.)

Sake

Sake is a Japanese rice beverage. Polished rice is soaked and steamed, and then it is inoculated with *Aspergillus oryzae*. This mixture is allowed to ferment for five to seven days, and then more water and *Saccharomyces* yeast are added. After an additional week of mixed fermentation, additional steamed rice, inoculated rice, and water are added in several stages, and the mixture continues to ferment for two to five weeks. The sake is strained and matured. Sake is typically 12 to 18 percent ABV, and a wide variety of styles and qualities are available.

Sima

Sima is a Finnish fermented lemonade. (For a recipe, see page 172.)

Smreka

Smreka is a fermented juniper berry beverage from Bosnia. Juniper berries are added to water and spontaneously fermented. The juniper berries float at the beginning; once they've all sunk to the bottom, the beverage is ready. This is a very low-alcohol beverage but could easily be made with sugar and champagne yeast or ale yeast for a fun and fast boozy variation.

Sweet Potato Fly

Sweet potato fly is spontaneously fermented sweet potato drink. For a boozy version, roast the sweet potatoes, add panela sugar, and use champagne yeast or ale yeast to ferment. Lemon, cinnamon, nutmeg, and ginger are possible flavor additions.

Tepache

Tepache is a fermented pineapple beverage that is native to Mexico. (For a recipe, see page 179.)

Toddy

Toddy is fermented palm sap, a version of which I drank in Cambodia. This beverage goes by many names, depending on where you are drinking it. It is common in Southeast Asia and Africa. It's usually spontaneously fermented for only a few days.

INGREDIENTS

Not all of the ingredients below are needed for every recipe. In fact, many are used only in one recipe. However, I want to discuss them briefly here, as quality and sourcing information may be helpful additions to the recipes.

Fruit

Fresh fruit is used in several of the recipes in this chapter. Try to obtain the ripest, highest-quality fruit that you can find. Organic fruit is optimal if available and within your budget.

Mauby Bark

Mauby bark is from a small tree in the buckthorn family. Mauby bark may be found at Caribbean and West Indian grocers. If you can't find mauby bark, another bark may be substituted; check your local herb and spice shop or international grocery for interesting edible barks.

Tea

Use a good-quality tea. It doesn't need to be the most expensive tea, but it should be fresh and flavorful. I have used everything from an Assam black tea to English breakfast tea for the Hong Kong Lemon Tea recipe.

Agave Nectar

Agave nectar is produced by processing agave juice. The juice is collected from the heart of the agave plant, then filtered and heated to produce simple sugars. Several

varieties of agave nectar are available: raw, light, amber, and dark. These are all fermentable and will contribute to the aroma and flavor of the fermented beverage. Generally speaking, the darker agave nectars will contribute more caramel notes in the finished beverage.

Rye Bread

One hundred percent rye bread is recommended for the kvass recipe. If you bake bread, this is the perfect opportunity to bake a 100 percent rye bread. Avoid highly processed breads with added oils, sugars, and processed flours. Other breads may be used, and if you fall in love with kvass, I would encourage you to experiment with breads using other grains or grains baked into other forms. The general rule is the less processed the bread, the better—look for breads that have whole ingredients and no preservatives.

Sugar

The majority of the recipes in this chapter call for less-processed sugars. Feel free to experiment with sugars; different sugars will contribute different aroma and flavor characteristics.

Yeast

I recommend champagne yeast for almost all of the recipes in this chapter. It's a fast, clean-fermenting yeast that tolerates a wide pH and temperature range and is very easy to measure out for small batches. Ale and wine yeasts may be used as well; my favorite beer yeast to use is an English ale yeast. English ale yeast may take a bit longer to ferment than champagne yeast but flocculates almost as well. However, almost all of the recipes in this chapter are based on beverages that are naturally fermented with indigenous yeast and bacteria. I encourage you to experiment with other commercial yeasts, including liquid and dry beer and wine yeasts and even bread yeast. If you have the interest and time, naturally fermenting many of these beverages with your native yeast and bacteria is definitely a worthwhile project.

HOW to MAKE FAR-FLUNG FERMENTS

Each of these beverages is different, but there is some common equipment you'll use for all of them. For detailed descriptions, see Chapter 1.

Materials
- 1-gal. wide-mouth glass jar with grommeted lid
- 1-gal. glass jug with appropriate size stopper
- Airlock
- Saucepan and/or teapot
- 4- or 8-c. heat-resistant glass pitcher
- Hydrometer
- Brewing notebook

SIMA

Vappu is the Finnish carnival celebrating May Day. Finns party in the streets and picnic in the parks to celebrate the beginning of spring. The traditional beverage imbibed during this nationwide celebration is sima, a refreshing low-alcohol lemon drink. Sima is typically made with fresh lemons, sugar, and bread yeast and allowed to ferment at room temperature for a day or two. The beverage is then bottled with raisins and placed in a cool spot. Once the raisins float, the sima is ready! There are many versions; sima originated as a mead, and honey-fermented varieties may be brewed. Fruits and berries are sometimes added, and there are modern versions brewed with other citrus fruits in place of the lemon. I use champagne yeast instead of the bread yeast to create a thirst-quenching alcoholic version of this traditional Finnish beverage. **Yield: *1 gallon***

- **1 gal. chlorine-free water**
- **1½ c. sugar (preferably white, but any combination of sugars may be used)**
- **3–4 lemons**
- **½ packet champagne yeast**
- **¹⁄₁₆ tsp. beer yeast nutrient**

Instructions:

1. Slice off and discard the pithy ends of the lemons. Thinly slice the remaining lemon.
2. Bring 3 cups of water to a boil.
3. Place the sliced lemons, 1½ cups of sugar, and beer yeast nutrient in a heat-resistant pitcher or saucepan. Pour the off-boil water over the lemon slices and sugar and stir until sugar is dissolved.
4. Steep for 5 to 10 minutes.
5. Cool the lemon-sugar mixture to below 80°F either in an ice bath or by adding chilled chlorine-free water.
6. Pour the lemon-sugar mixture into the sanitized wide-mouth jar. (Do not strain out lemons.) Top off with chlorine-free water to 1 gallon and stir to combine.
7. You may take a gravity reading using a hydrometer or refractometer at this point if you choose. The OG should be in the 1.032 to 1.036 range.

8. Pitch ½ packet of champagne yeast and top with a grommeted lid and filled airlock.

9. Ferment for 4 to 7 days at 65°F to 80°F.

10. Bottle as instructed on pages 26 to 31.

Variations

- **Sima Rosa:** Add ⅛ cup dried hibiscus flowers, also called Jamaica, with the lemon slices and sugar. Jamaica can often be found in Mexican, Latin American, or Caribbean stores or those sections of grocery stores. You can also find prepackaged hibiscus tea in the tea aisle. Hibiscus enhances the tartness of the lemons and adds wonderful fruit and floral notes. It also turns the sima a lovely shade of rose, making this a sophisticated hard pink lemonade.

- **Lavender Sima:** Add ½ tablespoon dried lavender flowers with the lemon slices and sugar. Inspired by a cocktail, the lavender adds a perfumed earthiness.

- **Mint Sima:** Add ¼ cup fresh mint leaves, 1 tablespoon dried mint, or 1 mint tea bag with the sliced lemons and sugar.

- **Mansikkasima (Strawberry):** Add ½ ounce of freeze-dried strawberries with the lemon slices and sugar. Strawberries and lemons are a classic pairing, and they dance beautifully in this version. And, like the Sima Rosa above, it's pink!

- **Raparperisima (Rhubarb):** Add ½ cup of fresh or frozen diced rhubarb with the lemon slices and sugar to brew a lovely spring beverage.

- **Greippisima (Grapefruit):** Substitute 1 sliced grapefruit for the lemon slices.

- **Traditional Sima:** Substitute bread yeast for the champagne yeast. Ferment at room temperature for 1 to 2 days then bottle, adding 2 to 3 raisins to each bottle. Refrigerate the bottles and drink the sima once the raisins float.

MAUBY

Mauby, also known as mavi, is a traditional beverage made in the Caribbean. It's based on the bark of the buckthorn shrub and is flavored with a variety of herbs and spices—the recipe varies from island to island. It may be served as an unfermented soda or allowed to spontaneously ferment for a few days. Either way, it is a lightly spiced cooling drink with a slightly bitter afternote. **Yield: *1 gallon***

- **1 gal. filtered, chlorine-free water**
- **2 c. panela sugar, grated**
- **5 g mauby bark**
- **2 g cinnamon (about ½ stick)**
- **1 small bay leaf**
- **1 g fresh rosemary (about 1 small sprig)**
- **½ tsp. dried marjoram**
- **1 star anise pod**
- **2 cloves**
- **1/16 tsp. fresh grated nutmeg**
- **1/8 tsp. fresh orange zest**
- **½ packet champagne yeast**
- **1/16 tsp. beer yeast nutrient**

Instructions

1. Bring 2 cups of water to a boil in a saucepan.
2. Add the mauby bark, cinnamon, bay leaf, rosemary, marjoram, anise, cloves, nutmeg, and orange zest to the boiling water. Simmer for 15 to 20 minutes.
3. Strain the spices out, return the spiced tea to the saucepan, and bring to a boil.
4. Once the tea is simmering, turn off the burner and add the yeast nutrient and panela sugar, stirring until completely dissolved.
5. Cool the mixture to below 80°F either in an ice bath or by adding chilled chlorine-free water.
6. Pour the mixture into a sanitized wide-mouth jar or jug, top off with chlorine-free water to 1 gallon, and stir to combine.
7. You may take a gravity reading using a hydrometer or refractometer at this point if you choose. The OG should be in the 1.038 to 1.042 range.
8. Pitch ½ packet of champagne yeast and top with a grommeted lid or stopper and filled airlock.
9. Ferment for 4 to 7 days at 65°F to 80°F.
10. Bottle as instructed on pages 26 to 31.

HONG KONG LEMON TEA

Sweetened lemon tea is a very popular beverage in Hong Kong, sold in every grocery and convenience store in the metropolitan area. When Hong Kong homebrewer Joshua Wolper first started brewing, he had a difficult time obtaining hops and barley, so he improvised with readily available ingredients and took inspiration from what the locals love. One of his unique fermented beverages was a lemon tea beer, and this beverage is based on his recipe. This is a delightful rejuvenating beverage, perfect for long, hot summer days. **Yield: *1 gallon***

- **1 gal. filtered, chlorine-free water**
- **14 black tea bags**
- **Zest and juice from 2 lemons**
- **1½ c. white sugar**
- **½ packet champagne yeast**
- **¹⁄₁₆ tsp. beer yeast nutrient**

Instructions

1. Bring 8 cups of water to a boil.
2. Pour over tea bags and steep for 10 minutes.
3. After 10 minutes, add beer yeast nutrient and sugar and stir to combine.
4. Add lemon juice and zest.
5. Cool the mixture to below 80°F either in an ice bath or by adding chilled chlorine-free water.
6. Pour the mixture into a sanitized wide-mouth jar or jug, top off with chlorine-free water to 1 gallon, and stir to combine.
7. You may take a gravity reading using a hydrometer or refractometer at this point if you choose. The OG should be in the 1.032 to 1.036 range.
8. Pitch ½ packet of champagne yeast and top with a grommeted lid or stopper and filled airlock.
9. Ferment for 4 to 7 days at 65°F to 80°F.
10. Bottle as instructed on pages 26 to 31.

Variations

- **Mint Tea:** Use 12 mint tea bags in place of the black tea. Lemon juice and zest may be added or eliminated, depending on preference.
- **Earl Grey Tea:** Substitute 10 bags of Earl Grey tea for the black tea and 1 teaspoon of fresh lemon zest for the juice and zest.
- **Jasmine Green Tea:** Use 12 jasmine green tea bags in place of the black tea and eliminate the lemon zest and juice. While this is one of the simplest beverages in the book, it is one of my favorite beverages. This is a surprisingly complex and delicious drink—the tannic earthiness of the green tea perfectly complements the delicate floral aroma and flavor.

TEPACHE

Tepache is a fermented pineapple drink originating in pre-Columbian Mexico. The traditional beverage is allowed to ferment naturally, resulting in a sweet, thirst-quenching beverage with alcohol below 1 percent ABV. It is often mixed with beer and served as a "beer cocktail." My version uses commercial yeast to produce a lightly sweet beverage around 4.5 percent ABV. **Yield: *1 gallon***

- **1 gal. filtered, chlorine-free water**
- **Rind from 1 pineapple (weight range of 350–440 g), cut into 2- to 3-inch pieces**
- **Small cinnamon stick**
- **3 cloves**
- **300 g piloncillo sugar**
- **½ packet champagne yeast**
- **¹⁄₁₆ tsp. beer yeast nutrient**

Instructions

1. Bring 2 cups of water to a boil.
2. Add cinnamon stick and cloves and steep for 10 minutes.
3. After 10 minutes, bring the solution to a simmer, turn off heat, add beer yeast nutrient and sugar, and stir to dissolve. Add pineapple rind.
4. Cool the mixture to below 80°F either in an ice bath or by adding chilled chlorine-free water.
5. Pour the mixture (including pineapple and spices) into a sanitized wide-mouth jar, top off with chlorine-free water to 1 gallon, and stir to combine.
6. You may take a gravity reading using a hydrometer or refractometer at this point if you choose. The OG should be around 1.04
7. Pitch ½ packet of champagne yeast and top with a grommeted lid and filled airlock.
8. Ferment for 4 to 7 days at 65°F to 80°F.
9. Bottle as instructed on pages 26 to 31.

KVASS

Kvass is a fermented bread beverage with origins in Eastern Europe. It was originally naturally fermented and contained less than 1 percent ABV. Modern kvass is often fermented with a yeast and bacteria starter that is kept going from batch to batch, similar to a sourdough starter. Kvass brewers are often very protective and proud of their starter cultures and can trace them back to previous generations. Kvass is served fresh in local establishments in many Eastern European countries as well as from kvass trucks or carts on sidewalks and street corners. I fell in love with kvass at a Russian bathhouse in Brooklyn. The proprietor of the establishment brews her kvass with a culture that has been in her family for years. **Yield: *1 gallon***

- **1 gal. filtered, chlorine-free water**
- **½ lb. crystal rye malt, finely crushed**
- **1 lb. 100% rye bread (no preservatives)**
- **1 c. panela sugar**
- **8 fresh mint leaves, roughly torn**
- **½ packet champagne yeast**
- **¹⁄₁₆ tsp. beer yeast nutrient**

Instructions

For complete brewing instructions, see pages 50–55.

1. Place crushed malt and rye bread into a brew bag. Heat 12 cups of water to 160°F to 168°F and add the bag of malt and bread. The steeping temperature should be 150°F to 166°F after adding the grain bag. Place in an oven and steep for 30 minutes.

2. After malt has steeped for 30 minutes, place the pot back on the stove, remove grain bag, and gently squeeze to drain.

3. Bring the wort to a boil. Once the boil is rolling, stir in the beer yeast nutrient and sugar, stirring to mix thoroughly and avoid scorching.

4. Boil for 10 minutes.

5. Remove from heat and add the mint.

6. Chill in an ice bath to just below 70°F.

7. Transfer to a sanitized fermentation vessel, add filtered water to top off to 1 gallon, and stir to combine.

8. Remove a sample to take a gravity reading, if desired. The gravity should be around 1.020.

9. Pitch the yeast.

10. Ferment at 65°F to 70°F. The fermentation should finish in 5 to 10 days. To bottle, follow master directions on page 27 to 31.

FAR-FLUNG FERMENTS

TAMARIND "PULQUE"

Pulque is an alcoholic beverage created by fermenting the sap of the agave, or maguey, plant. It dates back more than 1,000 years and was considered a sacred drink in pre-Columbian Mexican societies, where it was consumed only during ritualistic ceremonies. It evolved over time to a more pedestrian beverage and is now served in pulquerías throughout Mexico. The traditional fermentation process is rather complex and utilizes a strain of bacteria as the primary fermentation species, resulting in a cloudy white, somewhat sour beverage that ranges in alcohol strength from 3 to 8 percent. As most of us have no access to fresh agave sap or the bacteria required to create true pulque, I created a recipe that utilizes agave nectar, a syrup created by processing agave juice. While this beverage is a far cry from the true pulque you would be served at a pulquería in Mexico City, it is delicious and has a spicy, peppery quality reminiscent of pulque and its distilled big brother, tequila. Pulquerías offer a variety of flavored pulques, so the recipes below use some traditional flavorings. **Yield: _1 gallon_**

- **1 gal. filtered, chlorine-free water**

- **3 oz. sweet-and-sour dried tamarind, chopped (If you cannot find sweet-and-sour tamarind, you can also use dried tamarind with a dash of salt and chili powder.)**

- **16 oz. agave nectar**

- **½ packet champagne yeast**

- **¹⁄₁₆ tsp. beer yeast nutrient**

Instructions

1. Bring 1 cup of chlorine-free water to a boil.
2. Pour off-boil water over the chopped tamarind and steep for 10 minutes to rehydrate.
3. After 10 minutes, add the agave nectar and yeast nutrient and stir to combine.
4. Cool the mixture to below 80°F either in an ice bath or by adding chilled chlorine-free water.
5. Pour the mixture into a sanitized wide-mouth jar, top off with chlorine-free water to 1 gallon, and stir to combine.
6. You may take a gravity reading using a hydrometer or refractometer at this point if you choose. The OG should be in the 1.036 to 1.040 range.

(continued on page 184)

(continued on page 184)

7. Pitch ½ packet of champagne yeast and top with a grommeted lid and filled airlock.
8. Ferment for 4 to 7 days at 65°F to 80°F.
9. Bottle as instructed on pages 26 to 31.

Variation
WATERMELON-MINT-LIME "PULQUE"

Pictured on page 164. **Yield: *1 gallon***

- **¾ gal. filtered, chlorine-free water**
- **4 c. fresh watermelon juice (Use a juicer or a blender and a strainer to obtain fresh juice.)**
- **¼ tsp. fresh lime zest**
- **6 fresh mint leaves, roughly torn**
- **6 oz. agave nectar**
- **½ packet champagne yeast**
- **1/16 tsp. beer yeast nutrient**

Instructions

1. Add watermelon juice, agave nectar, lime zest, mint leaves, and yeast nutrient to a sanitized 1-gallon wide-mouth jar.
2. Add filtered water to reach 1 gallon and stir to combine thoroughly.
3. You may take a gravity reading using a hydrometer or refractometer at this point if you choose. The OG should be in the 1.038 to 1.042 range.
4. Pitch the yeast and top with a grommeted lid and filled airlock.
5. Ferment for 4 to 7 days at 65°F to 80°F.
6. Bottle as instructed on pages 26 to 31.

DEVELOPING YOUR OWN
FAR-FLUNG FERMENTS

THERE ARE TWO main approaches to designing your own fast far-flung fermentations. The first is to recreate a beverage that is indigenous to another part of the world and the second is to create a unique beverage using ingredients that are local to your area. If you'd like to recreate a beverage, start with the fermented beverage list in this chapter or do some research online or in your local library. How have others made this beverage? Start with a small batch, perhaps half a gallon, take copious notes, and go from there. If you'd like to make a novel drink, begin with the ingredients. What is starchy or sugary and grown, collected, or produced locally? Should you combine a few local ingredients? How have others prepared these ingredients for fermentation? And again, start with a small batch, take copious notes, and get your fermentation on. I highly recommend Sandor Ellix Katz's books, *Wild Fermentation* and *The Art of Fermentation*, for wonderful inspiration and recipe starting points. There are other books, both in print and out of print, that focus on fermenting local flora into beverages, primarily wine, but the recipes inside can easily be adapted to faster, lower-alcohol beverages. Far-flung fermentations are a fantastic way to explore the world or your neighborhood—in the form of a glass!

RESOURCES

BREWING & FERMENTATION EQUIPMENT & INGREDIENTS

Your local homebrew shop is probably your best resource for brewing beer and likely a good source for making many of the other beverages in this book. Not only does your local homebrew supplier sell supplies, they can answer your questions, offer suggestions, and are usually willing to offer feedback on the beverages that you brew.

If you don't have a local shop or are seeking ingredients or supplies that your local shop doesn't carry, check out the online homebrew and fermentation suppliers below.

Austin Homebrew Supply	austinhomebrew.com
Cultures for Health	culturesforhealth.com
Farmhouse Brewing Supply	farmhousebrewingsupply.com
Keystone Homebrew Supply	keystonehomebrew.com
Kombucha Brooklyn	kombuchabrooklyn.com
Midwest Brewing Supplies	midwestsupplies.com
MoreBeer!	morebeer.com
Northern Brewer	northernbrewer.com
Rebel Brewer	rebelbrewer.com
William's Home Brewing	williamsbrewing.com
Yemoos	yemoos.com

Ingredients

International grocery stores: Stores that specialize in one region of the world, international groceries, and groceries with large international aisles carry a wealth of ingredients for the recipes in this book. Look for interesting juices, sugars, teas, herbs, spices, fruits, and more in these stores. Remember, almost anything with a sugar or sugar source and no preservatives can be fermented!

Local farmers or green markets: Excellent sources for local produce as well as honey, herbs, and spices.

Tea, herb, and spice shops: These are fantastic sources for flavorings for your fermented beverages. I seek these out on my travels as teas and dried herbs and spices are lightweight and easy to pack in your luggage.

Trader Joe's: If you're lucky enough to live near a Trader Joe's, they stock an array of affordable and interesting ingredients, including freeze-dried fruit, dried fruit, teas, and juices.

Adagio Teas	adagio.com
Mighty Leaf Tea	mightyleaf.com
Monterey Bay Spice Company	herbco.com
Mountain Rose Herbs	mountainroseherbs.com
San Francisco Herb Co.	sfherb.com
Teavana	teavana.com

BOOKS

Beer Brewing

Beechum, Drew and Denny Conn. *Experimental Homebrewing: Breaking the Rules to Brew Great Beer*. Minneapolis, MN: Voyageur Press, 2014.

Hieronymus, Stan. *Brewing with Wheat: The "Wit" and "Weizen" of World Wheat Beer Styles*. Boulder, CO: Brewers Publications, 2010.

Mosher, Randy. *Radical Brewing: Recipes, Tales and World-Altering Meditations in a Glass*. Boulder: Brewers Publications, 2004.

Palmer, John J. *How to Brew: Everything You Need to Know to Brew Beer Right the First Time*. Boulder: Brewers Publications, 2006.

Papazian, Charlie. *The Complete Joy of Homebrewing, Fourth Edition*. New York: William Morrow, 2014.

———. *The Homebrewer's Companion Second Edition: The Complete Joy of Homebrewing, Master's Edition*. New York: William Morrow, 2014.

Tonsmeire, Michael. *American Sour Beer: Innovative Techniques for Mixed Fermentations*. Boulder: Brewers Publications, 2014.

Zainasheff, Jamil, and John Palmer *Brewing Classic Styles: 80 Winning Recipes Anyone Can Brew*. Boulder: Brewers Publications, 2007.

Other Fermented Beverages

Buhner, Stephen Harrod. *Sacred and Herbal Healing Beers: The Secrets of Ancient Fermentation*. Boulder, CO: Siris Books, 1998.

Childs, Eric and Jessica. *Kombucha!: The Amazing Probiotic Tea That Cleanses, Heals, Energizes, and Detoxifies*. New York: Avery, 2013.

Christensen, Emma. *True Brews: How to Craft Fermented Cider, Beer, Sake, Soda, Mead, Kefir, and Kombucha at Home*. New York: Ten Speed Press, 2013.

Jolicoeur, Claude. *The New Cider Maker's Handbook: A Comprehensive Guide for Craft Producers*. White River Junction, VT: Chelsea Green Publishing, 2013.

Katz, Sandor Ellix. *The Art of Fermentation: An In-Depth Exploration of Essential Concepts and Processes from around the World*. White River Junction, VT: Chelsea Green Publishing, 2012.

———. *Wild Fermentation: The Flavor, Nutrition, and Craft of Live-Culture Foods*. White River Junction, VT: Chelsea Green Publishing, 2003.

Lee, Stephen, and Ken Koopman. *Kombucha Revolution: 75 Recipes for Homemade Brews, Fixers, Elixirs, and Mixers*. New York: Ten Speed Press, 2013.

Mansfield, Scott. *Strong Waters: A Simple Guide to Making Beer, Wine, Cider and Other Spirited Beverages at Home*. New York: The Experiment, 2010.

Schloss, Andrew. *Homemade Soda: 200 Recipes for Making and Using Fruit Sodas and Fizzy Juices, Sparkling Waters, Root Beers & Cola Brews, Herbal and Healing Waters, Sparkling Teas & Coffees, Shrubs & Switchels, Cream Sodas & Floats and Other Carbonated Concoctions*. North Adams, MA: Storey Publishing, 2011.

Schramm, Ken. *The Compleat Meadmaker: Home Production of Honey Wine from Your First Batch to Award-winning Fruit and Herb Variations*. Boulder: Brewers Publications, 2003.

Vargas, Pattie, and Rich Gulling. *Making Wild Wines and Meads: 125 Unusual Recipes Using Herbs, Fruits, Flowers and More*. North Adams, MA: Storey Publishing, 1999.

ACKNOWLEDGMENTS

I am grateful for so many people that have inspired and encouraged me in my journey through brewing and fermentation.

Most of all, a very special thanks to Chris Cuzme, who helped out in so many ways throughout the creation of this book. I couldn't ask for a better partner in brewing and life!

A special thanks also to my parents, Sue and Jim Izett, and my brother, John Izett, for being so incredibly supportive.

This book would not have been possible without my editor, Thom O'Hearn, and my photographer, Michael Harlan Turkell. Thanks to Drew Beechum for getting this whole project started and for the encouragement along the way.

Thanks to all of the homebrewers that taught and inspired me in the early days: Sean White, Ray Girard, Phil Clarke, John Naegele, Ron Carlson, Chris Post, Vlad Kowalyk, Dave Witzel, and everyone in my BJCP class.

A huge thanks to Bill Coleman for gifting me my original all-grain brewing system and Ron Carlson for being my backyard brewing partner.

Thanks to my local homebrew shops, Brooklyn Homebrew and Bitter & Esters, and all of their employees who helped me over the development of this book. Big props to BK Homebrew owners Danielle Cefaro and Benjamin Stutz and B&E owners John LaPolla and Doug Amport for everything they do for the NYC homebrewing community!

Thanks to everyone in the New York City craft beer and brewing community who has influenced, motivated, or encouraged me in one way or another: Warren Becker, Mike Lovullo, Patrick Donagher, Josh Bernstein, Jimmy Carbone, Jon Voris, Jess Molinari, Stephen Durley, Hayley Jensen, Jonathan Moxey, Lee Jacobson, Zack Kinney, Ken Hettinger, Ken Munno, Steve Lander, Chris McNally, Harlie Levine, Oskar Norlander, Ed Kurowski, Chris Pagnotta, Chris Prout, Chris Strait, Alex Hall, B. R. Rolya, everyone who has ever shared their homebrew with me, and many, many more. Thanks to Annika Ginsberg for understanding and supporting.

INDEX

ABOUT the AUTHOR

Mary Izett is a passionate homebrewer specializing in fast and alternatively fermented beverages. She co-hosts Fuhmentaboudit!, a live weekly show on all things fermentable on Heritage Radio Network. She is a nationally ranked beer judge in the Beer Judging Certification Program. She has been the president of both the New York City Homebrewer Guild and the Malted Barley Appreciation Society and has written for *Ale Street News*, *All About Beer*, and *Zymurgy*.

First published in 2015 by Voyageur Press, an imprint of Quarto Publishing Group USA Inc., 400 First Avenue North, Suite 400, Minneapolis, MN 55401 USA

The information in this book is true and complete to the best of our knowledge. All recommendations are made without any guarantee on the part of the author or Publisher, who also disclaims any liability incurred in connection with the use of this data or specific details.

We recognize, further, that some words, model names, and designations mentioned herein are the property of the trademark holder. We use them for identification purposes only. This is not an official publication.

Voyageur Press titles are also available at discounts in bulk quantity for industrial or sales-promotional use. For details write to Special Sales Manager at Quarto Publishing Group USA Inc., 400 First Avenue North, Suite 400, Minneapolis, MN 55401 USA.

To find out more about our books, visit us online at www.voyageurpress.com.

ISBN: 978-0-7603-4737-9

Library of Congress
Cataloging-in-Publication Data

Izett, Mary, 1972-
Speed brewing : techniques and recipes for fast-fermenting beers, ciders, meads, and more / Mary Izett.
    pages cm
Includes index.
ISBN 978-0-7603-4737-9 (paperback)
1. Brewing—Amateurs' manuals. I. Title.
TP570.I94 2015
663'.42--dc23
                        2014044807

Acquisitions Editor: Thom O'Hearn
Project Manager: Madeleine Vasaly
Art Director: Cindy Samargia Laun
Cover and Book Design: Brad Norr
Book Design and Layout: Diana Boger

Stock credits: front cover, MaraZe/Shutterstock; p. 45, Dimitar Sotirov/Shutterstock; p. 94, Bogdan Wankowicz/Shutterstock; p. 97, Christopher Elwell/Shutterstock

Printed in China

10 9 8 7 6 5 4 3 2 1